God and Me! 2 ®

Ages 6-9

God and Me! 2®

Ages 6-9

Diane Cory

*To my mother Mary for her many hours of typing and
praying for me during the writing of this book.*

*Also, to my husband Scott who has always been a source
of strength and encouragement to me.*

GOD AND ME!® 2 FOR AGES 6-9
© 2015 by Diane Cory

Published by Rose Kidz®
an imprint of Hendrickson Publishing Group
Rose Publishing, LLC
P.O. Box 3473
Peabody, Massachusetts 01961-3473 USA
www.hendricksonpublishinggroup.com

Cover Illustrator: Phyllis Harris
Interior Illustrator: Aline L. Heiser

ISBN: 978-1-58411-055-2
#L46828
RoseKidz Reorder #110554
Juvenile Nonfiction / Religion / Devotion & Prayer

*Printed in United States of America
Printed January 2021*

Table of Contents

Table of Contents

Introduction

Hey, Girls! A piece of candy is just as sweet the second time around, right? I pray **God & Me! 2** will be just as sweet to you the second time around. God's Word is always sweet because it tells us about His love and kindness. As you read God's Word, let it melt in your heart and mind. Let God teach you as you read **God & Me! 2** and work through the awesome activities.

This edition is power-packed with even more prayer lessons, puzzles, and activities. Allow each prayer lesson to fire you up to talk more often with God. You'll also learn to be a girl for God as Jochebed, Hannah, Anna, Esther and others were. Of course, there's always more to learn about Jesus, too. You'll also read about God's "wardrobe" and how to be the best-dressed girl in town!

Don't Forget...

 You can read the devotionals in this book whenever you want and in whatever order you like.

 Each devotion has a topic and a Scripture. Try to memorize the Scripture!

 There's a story and some questions to answer.

 After your prayer, take a look at the activity. The projects and puzzles will help you act on what you've just learned. At the back of the book you will find answers to the puzzles.

May **God & Me! 2** point you toward **making right choices and growing closer to Jesus!**

Power-packed God

A Powerful Love

God's love for me is powerful.

Show the wonder of your great love.

~ Psalm 17:7

God's Princess Bride

Kaley watched as her big sister, Carrie, entered the room in her wedding dress. "Wow!" exclaimed Kaley. "You look like a princess!"

Carrie smiled at Kaley, "I feel like a princess today, little sis! I can't wait to marry Mike, my bridegroom and prince."

Their mother placed a wedding veil over Carrie's head and face. "I want to be a princess bride someday, too," said Kaley.

"You'll be a bride even if you don't get married," said her mom.

"What do you mean?" asked Kaley.

"When you come to know Jesus you become like his bride," her mom explained. "The Bible says that God designed a husband and wife to be tied together in powerful love. God has that kind of powerful love for us. God's design for people is to grow closer in friendship with him. Our sin breaks that friendship with God. But God never gives up on his purposes for us. He sent Jesus to die for our sins. Once our sins are forgiven, we can know our groom: Jesus."

"I get it!" said Kaley. "God chose weddings and brides to show us that he wants to come close to us."

"That's exactly right," her mom told her as she smiled and hugged her daughters. "As his brides, we should always listen to his Word and choose to follow his ways. That's what will help us to grow in his powerful love for us."

Your Turn

1. Why do you think Kaley wanted to be a bride?

_____

_____

2. How does being God's bride make you feel about yourself?

_____

_____

Prayer

Dear God, thank you for sending Jesus to take away my sin. I am grateful that You are my bridegroom. You make me feel special and pretty. Your powerful love makes me feel like a princess. Your powerful love is all I need. Amen.

Heart Puzzle

Solve the puzzle in the heart below.

1 2 3 4 5 6 7 8 9 10 11 12 13 14 15 16 17 18 19 20 21 22 23 24 25 26
A B C D E F G H I J K L M N O P Q R S T U V W X Y Z

$$\overline{}_{7}\ \overline{}_{15}\ \overline{}_{4}\quad \overline{}_{12}\ \overline{}_{15}\ \overline{}_{22}\ \overline{}_{5}\ \overline{}_{19}\quad \overline{}_{13}\ \overline{}_{5}!$$

The answer is on page 238.

Beautiful Trust

My God can be trusted.

I have trusted in the LORD and have not faltered.

~ Psalm 26:1

The Ring and Ax

Jamie and her mom were washing the pots and pans. Jamie stood on a stool and washed while Mom dried.

As Jamie washed, she looked at the bright stone in her new ring. Mom had told her, "You'd better take off your ring to wash pans." But Jamie never had a ring before and she didn't want to remove it.

When Jamie finished washing, she looked at her finger. The ring was gone!

"I've lost my ring," cried Jamie. "It must have slipped off my finger."

"Let's check the soapy water," said Mom.

"Maybe it will float to the top of the water," Jamie said hopefully.

"I think it's too heavy to float, honey," said Mom. "But let's trust God to help us find it."

Jamie moved her hand around in the dirty dishwater and something shiny floated to the top.

"Here it is! Here it is!" she shouted. "My ring, my ring, my beautiful ring!"

"See, God can be trusted even when it comes to your ring," said Mom.

In Bible times, people trusted God, too. For example, in 2 Kings chapter 6 you can read about some men who were cutting down trees at the river. As one man worked, the sharp end of his ax fell off the handle and into the river.

"Oh no!" cried the man. "That ax isn't mine! It belongs to someone else and I must find it."

The men called out to Elisha, God's prophet, and said, "Come and help us find the ax."

Elisha cut a stick and threw it into the water. It landed right where the ax had fallen. The iron ax suddenly rested on top of the water.

"Lift it out!" said Elisha. The man picked the ax out of the water. Elisha showed the man that God cared about his lost ax. Put your trust in God because he cares for you. You can trust God to help you.

Your Turn

How can you help others learn to trust in God and Jesus?

_____

_____

Prayer

Dear God, I can trust You in everything. There is nothing too big or too small for You. Help me to trust You enough to ask for help even when I lose something. Amen.

Soapy Puzzle

Find and circle the ring in the dish soap. At the bottom of the page, write what you can trust God for in your life.

I will trust God and Jesus to _____.

The Plowman's Power

God's Word powerfully guides me.

It's hard for you to kick against the goads.

~ Acts 26:14

God's Goad

"What's a goad?" Tracy asked her mom as she looked at her spelling list.

"A goad is a stick with a sharp point on the end!" said Mom. "In Bible times, farmers used the goad to keep their oxen in the planting rows. If a young ox didn't like its planting job, it would walk out of the row. Then the plowman would poke the ox with the tip of the goad. The stick then caused the ox great pain."

"Oh!" said Tracy. "It's like the time we planted carrots together in the garden. I kept wanting to go play with my friends rather than do the job."

"Kind of!" said Mom, laughing.

"It's more like this, honey," Mom continued. "The Bible tells of a man named Saul. He was on the road to Damascus. Jesus appeared to him because he was harassing Christians. Jesus said, 'Saul, Saul, why do you work against My people and Me? It's hard for you to kick against the goads.' Jesus was saying it's no use to go against God's guidance and power in our lives."

Mom put her arm around Tracy. "Saul was pushing against God's guidance in his life. He was pushing God away when God wanted his attention. God wants our attention, too! He uses his Word and his Spirit as goads. When we start to make wrong choices he guides us back. The Bible has God's power to prick at our hearts and minds. That's what keeps us doing right."

"I get it!" said Tracy. "Goads are good!"

Kicking against the goad is pushing away God's guiding power. It's pushing away his Word, and his Spirit. There's power in God's Word!

Your Turn

1. The goad caused pain for the ox. How does sin cause pain in your life?

_____

_____

2. How can God's Word be a goad in your life?

_____

_____

Prayer

Dear God, keep me from kicking against the goads. Help me to allow you to guide and direct my life. Teach me to obey Your Word and my parents. Amen.

The Goad Secret

The Bible is God's power to poke your heart and mind. Decode the goads below.
The secret tells what not to do when God uses his goad in your life.

A	B	C	D	E	F	G	H	I	J
1	2	3	4	5	6	7	8	9	10

K	L	M	N	O	P	Q	R	S	T
11	12	13	14	15	16	17	18	19	20

U	V	W	X	Y	Z				
21	22	23	24	25	26				

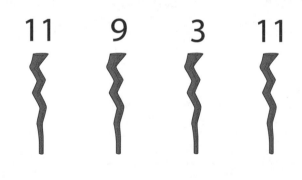

4　15　14　20

____ ____ ____ ____

11　9　3　11

____ ____ ____ ____

The answer is on page 238.

Come Closer, God!

I'm God's friend.

Let us draw near to God with a sincere heart.

~Hebrews 10:22

Let God Pass By...

Kayla liked Angie from the day she met her. It was the first day of second grade. Kayla wanted to get close to Angie and make friends. But Angie had a lot of other friends. She was outgoing and everyone liked her.

"Mom, I met a girl named Angie. I want to be her friend, but I'm just not sure how to do that," Kayla told her mom. "She has so many friends. I feel like she doesn't even see me."

"Well, honey, you just need to be friendly and be yourself. Maybe you can invite her over this Saturday," said Mom.

"That's a good idea, Mom!" said Kayla.

Just as Kayla was looking to make Angie her friend, God is looking for people to be his friend. He is waiting for you to grow closer to him. God longs for you to invite him into your life. God has secrets he wants to tell you!

Moses was God's friend. "I'll tell you my secrets because you're my friend," God told Moses. "Come closer to me, but you can't see my face. No one can see my face or he or she will die. Stand in a dent of a rock and as I pass by I'll put my hand over you. After I go by, I'll take my hand away. Then you'll only see my back."

God wanted Moses to come closer to him. God wants you to come closer, too! Let God pass by you... today.

Your Turn

1. Do you think God wants you to know him as Moses did? Why or why not?

_____

_____

2. What are some things you can do that will help you move closer to God?

_____

_____

Prayer

Dear God, come closer to me. I want to know you and be your friend as Moses was. You are a powerful God, but I know you love and care for me. Thank you, God! Amen.

God's Cave Girl

List in the cave some things that will help you draw closer to God. Then fill in the missing words in the verse below.

Let us draw _____ to God with a sincere _____.

The answer is on page 238.

Sharing Is Sweet

I should share with others.

Do not forget to do good and to share with others.

~ Hebrews 13:16

Give Me Five

"Give me five!" Amy told Suzie in the school lunchroom one day.

Suzie held her hand in the air to meet Amy's.

Amy laughed. "I don't want to slap your hand. I want five of your crackers."

Mini graham crackers with chocolate frosting were the most popular treat at the girls' lunch table. Nearly everyone had them in their lunches. But Amy's mom would only allow her take graham crackers in her lunch once a week. So Amy was hoping Suzie would share her crackers with Amy.

Suzie thought for a moment about her friend's request. Then she began to count her crackers.

One, two, three, four, five, six, seven, eight, nine! I have nine left, she thought. *If I give away five, I'll only have four for myself.*

Then Suzie thought of something her Sunday school teacher had read to her class from the Bible: "Do not forget to do good and to share with others." Her teacher also had said, "We should share with happy hearts because God gives to us with a happy heart."

Then Suzie remembered a story in the Bible about a boy who shared his lunch with Jesus. Jesus took that boy's small lunch of five rolls and two fish and fed 5,000 people with it!

If that boy can share his lunch, then I can share five crackers with my friend, Suzie thought. So that's just what she did!

"Here's five!" Suzie said as she placed the crackers on Amy's napkin.

Then Amy said, "Here's five!" as she thankfully lifted her hand for Suzie to clap. "Next time I have crackers, I'll share mine with you!"

Your Turn

1. Why do you think God wants you to share?

_____

_____

2. How can you remind yourself to share with others?

_____

_____

Prayer

Dear God, show me how to share with a happy heart. Soften my heart so I desire to share with others. Amen.

Here's Five!

Think of five people with whom you can share something. Write a name on the line by each finger below. Can you give them a high five?

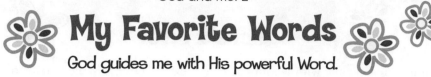

My Favorite Words

God guides me with His powerful Word.

For the word of God is alive and active.

~ Hebrews 4:12

Words of Power

Jackie loved playing with most of the girls on her block. But there was one girl who made her feel bad: Mary Jane. She was a bully who picked on Jackie because Jackie loved Jesus.

"There is no God!" Mary Jane would say with a mean voice. "Little goody-two-shoes! What good is your Jesus to me anyway?"

Jackie's mother had been teaching her Bible verses. One day when Mary Jane was taunting Jackie, those Bible verses made her feel bold for Jesus.

"Why do you pick on Jesus?" she asked Mary Jane. "Jesus loves you and died for you, even though you say mean words about him. In the Bible it says, 'God has loved you with an everlasting love.'"

Mary Jane was shocked at what Jackie said. She suddenly began to cry. Jackie felt sorry for Mary Jane, so she put her arm around her. When Mary Jane stopped crying, she asked Jackie to tell her more about Jesus. Then she said she would never bully Jackie again.

There is great power in God's Word! God's Word causes people to see how much He loves them. God's powerful Word causes people to see their sin, and it heals their hearts.

Can you speak the powerful words of God? Learn God's Word as Jackie did and speak it wisely when you feel God's leading.

Your Turn

1. What are some powerful words you know from the Bible?

_____

_____

2. Why do you think God's words are so powerful?

_____

_____

Prayer

Dear God, I am thankful for your words of power and truth. Teach me your Word, Lord, so I can say powerful words to help people know you. Amen.

Powerful Messages

On the bulletin board below, write your own powerful message telling God how much you love him.

Powerful Father

I can tell friends about my powerful God.

Sing praise to him; tell of all his wonderful acts.

~ Psalm 105:2

Power Over the Sky

"My God is powerful," said Rachel to Alison.

"Who is God?" asked Alison.

"He is my Father in heaven, and e is very powerful," replied Rachel.

Rachel loved telling her friends about her powerful Father in heaven.

A Bible-times man named Joshua knew the power of his Father in heaven, too. Joshua led a big army.

One time, Joshua had to fight five armies in one battle! God told him, "Don't be afraid. I'll help you win."

Joshua's army marched all night to surprise the king's armies. God helped Joshua's army as he promised by causing big hailstones to fall from the sky. The hailstones fell right on the heads of Joshua's enemies! Joshua's army chased the enemy backward.

Then Joshua prayed to God, "Let the sun stand still." God made the sun stand still and the moon also stopped moving. The sun didn't move for one whole day. That gave Joshua's army more daylight to fight and win.

God's people took the land that day. The Bible tells about many other powerful acts of God. "Powerful" means mighty, strong, forceful and able to do anything. That is our God! He has the ability to do great and big acts if he chooses.

Be like Rachel and tell your friends about your powerful God.

Your Turn

1. How do God's powerful ways surprise you?

_____

_____

2. How does God show his power in your life?

_____

_____

Prayer

Dear God, thank you for your power. I like the way you are both powerful and kind. Show me how to tell others of your wonderful acts. Amen.

God's Power Dots

Connect the power dots below! Write your friend's names inside the pictures. Make plans to tell them about your powerful God.

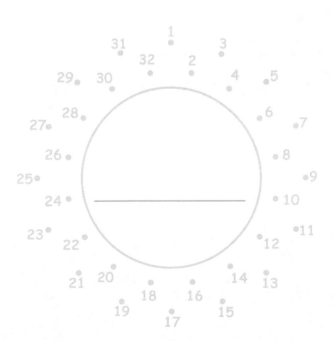

Powerful News

Jesus was sent from a powerful God.

I am the LORD, the God of all mankind.
Is anything too hard for me?

~ Jeremiah 32:27

Postcard Madness

Jenny loved traveling! Each winter break she and her parents vacationed in a warm place. Every year they chose a different beach to explore.

Jenny's favorite part of the trips was collecting postcards. She sent cards to all of her friends because she couldn't wait until she got home to tell them the news from her trip!

Dad teased Jenny and said, "This is postcard madness!"

"It's not madness, Daddy!" said Jenny. "It's gladness! I'm so glad to share the good news from my trip that I just can't wait until we get home to spread the news."

You can have the same kind of madness and gladness about the Bible when you share God's powerful news! What's the news? It's the message of the Bible: God's love for us and for all people. It's the news that Jesus wants to have a personal friendship with each of us.

Because Jesus died, our sins can be forgiven. He overcame death so we can live forever with God. Jesus' life and death should create in us a desire to tell our friends. This is news that is worth telling! Jenny couldn't wait to get home and share the good news of her trip. When will you share God's most powerful Good News? Let it be today!

Your Turn

1. Why is the Good News important to share?

_____

_____

2. Can you think of some ways God may want you to share His powerful news?

_____

_____

Prayer

Dear God, thank you for the Good News about Jesus. Thank you, God, for using your power to send Jesus to rule over the earth. Amen.

My Madness Card

Write a postcard to a friend, telling her or him about God's powerful news.

My God Is Great

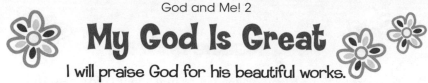

I will praise God for his beautiful works.

How great are your works, LORD!

~ Psalm 92:5

Stories of the Beautiful

Kelly went with her parents on an airplane. The plane flew over some beautiful sights.

"Look, there's the Grand Canyon," said Mom. "Our God is great to make such beauty."

"How many beautiful things has God made?" Kelly asked.

"Oh, we could never count them all because there are so many," said Dad.

"Can we try?" Kelly stuck her nose against her window in the plane. "After all, we can see everything from up here."

"Okay," said Dad, "let's look out the window and count the beautiful things God has made."

Jessica's father loved to study the stars. One summer night Jessica and Dad looked at the moon. They used special glasses to make the moon look closer.

"You can see the craters," said Dad. "God is great to make something so wonderful!"

Sophie and her little brother, Josh, played in the falling snow. They tried to catch the snow on their tongues.

"My teacher told me that each snowflake is different," Sophie told Josh.

"Wow!" said Josh. "God must be really powerful to make each snowflake different."

Everywhere you look, you see God's great works. Kelly, Jessica and Sophie all saw God's creation. Praise God each day for his beautiful works.

Your Turn

1. What do you think is one of God's greatest works?

_____

_____

2. Why should we praise God for his great works?

_____

_____

Prayer

Dear God, thank you for your power and greatness. I praise you for your power. I see it in the world around me. You are a great God. Amen.

Creation Story Squares

Look at the creation story squares below. Each day this week, thank God for the creation work in that square. For example, on Sunday, you could say, "Thank you, God, for the trees. You are a great God!"

A Perfect and Holy God

God's power helps me to do what's right.

"Be holy, because I am holy!"

~ 1 Peter 1:16

It's Perfect!

"What do you think of this dress, Mom?" asked Kara. Kara and her mother loved to shop together.

"Kara, honey, it's perfect," Mom said as Kara twirled in front of her.

Sally's mom fixed Sally's hair each day before school. Her mom combed her shiny brown hair and placed a bow behind her left ear.

"That's perfect," Sally said to her mom as she looked into the mirror.

Brittany's dad was calling for her. "Help me hang this picture on the wall, Brit," he said. "Tell me if I need to move it to the left or right."

"Okay," said Brittany. "Now move it down just a little...and stop. That's perfect!"

We call something "perfect" when it looks right to us. Did you know everything is right about God? He is the only one who is perfect. He is called "holy." That means he is perfect in every way. God never makes a mistake.

1 Peter 1:16 says, "Be holy, because I am holy." That means you should always try to do the right thing. As you keep yourself away from sin, you stay close to God. Then you are on your way to becoming holy for God.

You will never be perfect as God is perfect. But wanting to do the right thing and trying your best is the way God wants you to live.

Your Turn

1. Why aren't you perfect?

_____

_____

2. Do you think God could ever do anything wrong? Why?

_____

_____

Prayer

Dear God, I'm glad you are holy and right. Please help me to do right and live the way you want for me. Amen.

A Holy Mirror

No one is as perfect as God is, but the Bible says to be holy and do what is right. Write on the mirror below what you do to keep from making wrong choices. For example: "Go to church," "Choose the right friends," and "Talk to God."

Real Love

I want to know God's real love.

Love comes from God.

~ 1 John 4:7

Powerful and Mighty Love

"Yuck, they kissed," said Kim as she flipped the TV channel. "Do those people love each other?"

"No," her mom told her. "They were just pretending. People on TV often pretend to be in love. The word 'love' is often used incorrectly."

"Like how?" asked Kim.

"Well, we sometimes say, 'I love ice cream,' 'I love roller skating' or 'I love to watch cartoons.' What we really mean is that we like those things a lot. Saying we love ice cream is different from saying we love our parents. It's different from God's love for us. God's love isn't just words. God's love has power in it. His love has the power to make us love others when we don't feel like it. His love has power to cause us to forgive hurts. His love has power to do good things. His love is just mighty!"

Kim thought for a minute. "So when God sent Jesus to die for our sins, that was real love, right, Mom?"

Mom nodded. "God gives us a home and a family and he helps us when we have problems–all of that is real love. God is so full of love that he can't hold it inside himself. It sort of spills out to people all over the world."

Kim laughed. "Now how about some of that ice cream I like a lot but don't really love?"

Your Turn

1. What kind of love has the most power?

_____

_____

2. What does God do to show real love?

_____

_____

3. How can a person know God's real love?

_____

_____

Prayer

Dear God, I know how full of love you are. I am glad you offer your love to the world. Help me to show real love to others. Amen.

Spilled Love

God has so much love for us that it spills out onto us. He wants to give us his powerful love. Write what God has done to show his love for you on the overflowing hearts below.

Father Knows Best

God knows what's best for me.

*For it is God who works in you to will and
to act according to his good purpose.*

~ Philippians 2:13

The Opposite News

Anna's mother arrived home from the hospital with Anna's new brother. Anna couldn't wait to hold him.

"He's so cute!" she said with joy.

The whole family was happy until the phone rang. Anna's dad hung up the phone with tears in his eyes.

"Grandma has cancer," said Dad.

"What's cancer?" asked Anna.

"Cancer is a bad sickness," said Dad. Dad wiped his eyes. "Grandma needs an operation."

"How odd," said Mom. "We have bad news on a good news day."

"But why did God let Grandma be sick on our special day?" asked Anna.

"I don't know, honey," said Dad. "But God knows and he is in control."

"That's true," agreed Mom. "God has a plan and is at work in this problem. Even when bad things happen, we feel his love. God is powerful and kind, in bad times and in good times. He knows what's best for us."

"Let's pray to God right now," said Dad.

Your Turn

1. Has something good and bad happened to you at the same time?

_____

_____

2. What should you do when good and bad happen together?

_____

_____

3. How will learning Philippians 2:13 make you feel about God?

_____

_____

Prayer

Dear God, I know you love me in good times and bad. Help me to trust you to have a plan. I know you are at work for my best. Thank you, God! Amen.

God Is At Work Puzzle

It is comforting to know that God is always at work to help us. Find and circle the words GOD IS AT WORK hidden in the letters below.

C	R	K	W	I	S	A
S	O	M	H	N	E	Y
G	O	N	I	N	Z	D
U	O	P	T	P	D	O
W	C	D	A	T	H	S
R	L	Q	K	J	O	T
W	O	R	K	Z	V	L

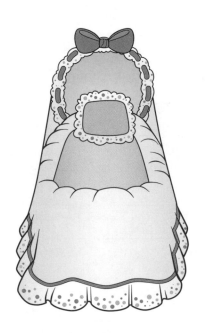

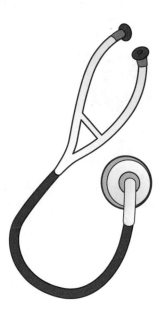

The answer is on page 238.

Powerful Patience

I know God cares for me.

Help the weak, be patient with everyone.

~ 1 Thessalonians 5:14

Bugging God

"Mom, Timmy keeps asking me to help him build blocks," said Mary. "He's bugging me!"

"Your little brother isn't trying to bug you," said Mom.

"But he talks too much," said Mary. "He's always talking about that dumb cartoon show he watches. I don't want to hear about it."

"Mary, you need patience. What if God thought we were bugging him? I'm glad God loves us enough to listen to us," said Mom.

The Bible says, "Help the weak, be patient with everyone." The Bible also says that God cares for those who trust in him. God is concerned about even the little things for which we pray. We are never "bugging" God when we talk to him about little things. He always has time and patience for us.

Timmy bothered Mary with questions and talking. We never bug God with anything. We can tell God anything and trust God every time! God has powerful patience while loving us.

Your Turn

1. Why do you think Mary was "bugged" by her little brother, Timmy?

_____

_____

2. Does anyone bug you? Who?

_____

_____

3. Why is it impossible for us to bug God?

_____

_____

Prayer

Thank you for caring about every part of my life. Help me not let people bug me. Thank you, God, for not being bugged by me. Amen.

Bugging Blocks

Try to "bug" God by telling him things you want him to know or do for you. Write something different on each block. You won't be able to bug a powerfully patient God!

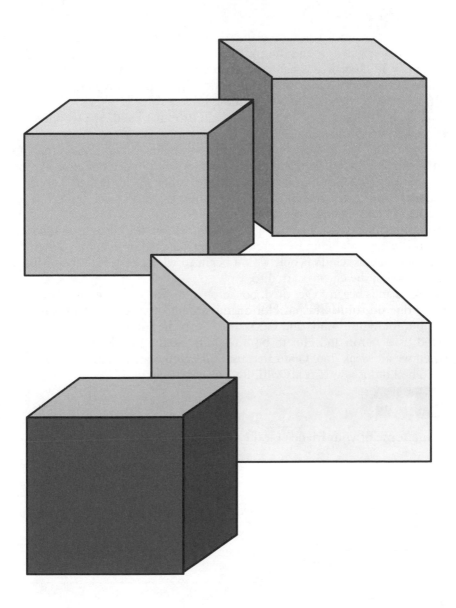

God, Give Me a Hand

God's power makes me strong.

For I am the LORD your God who takes hold of your
right hand and says to you, Do not fear; I will help you.

~ Isaiah 41:13

Hands Up

"Raise your hand if you have a question," Mrs. Colby told her second grade class. "I'll answer you as soon as I can."

One day in class, Kelly's hand went up but Mrs. Colby didn't see her. Kelly's hand was in the air for a long time. She couldn't hold it up any longer.

My arm feels like it will fall off, she thought.

Finally, her name was called and she could drop her hand. She wondered if the question was worth the pain!

What if you had to hold up both your hands for a long time? Once, God's friend Moses had to do just that. But it wasn't to wait to ask a question. An enemy army came to fight against God's people. Moses called for his helper, Joshua.

"Choose some men and take them out to fight," Moses said. "I'll stand on the top of the hill tomorrow as you fight."

So Joshua took the men out to fight. Moses went up the hill as he said he would. His friends, Aaron and Hur, went, too. They all watched from above. When Moses held up both hands, God's people would begin to win the battle. When Moses put his hands down, the enemy started to win.

Moses' hands began to get tired. So Aaron and Hur sat Moses on a rock. Aaron stood on one side of Moses and Hur on the other. They held his hands high from morning until night. Joshua and God's army won the battle!

God used Aaron and Hur to be his hands, holding up Moses. God holds us up when we are weak, too. God often uses others to be strong for us and to be his hands. The Lord is always ready with his power to help us.

Your Turn

1. Name some of your friends God can use to help you.

_____

_____

2. Think of a time when you were weak and needed God's help. Did he hold you up?

_____

_____

Prayer

God, your power is great! You are my helper. Help me to trust in you when I am weak. Amen.

Arm Writing

Who has God used to help you do something special? Try to think of two people. Write their names on the girl's arm below. Pray and thank God for your own "Aaron" and "Hur."

Powerful Deeds

I know God's power is wonderful.

Great and mighty God…great are your
purposes and mighty are your deeds.

~ Jeremiah 32:18-19

The Fountain

Lora was spending the weekend with her Aunt Carol while her parents were away. One night, a big storm blew in. Lightning struck close by and the lights went out in Aunt Carol's house.

"I have an oil lamp," she told Lora. "Let's get the oil and fill the lamp."

They filled the lamp with oil and then lit it. Sitting in the light of the oil lamp, they talked.

"I'm scared," said Lora

"The power of a storm can be scary," replied Aunt Carol, "but God's power is greater than any storm."

Lora snuggled in close next to her aunt. "God's power is wonderful," Aunt Carol added. "The Bible tells many stories of God's wonderful power."

"Tell me one," said Lora.

"Well, the first missionary, Paul, traveled to many places telling others about Jesus. Once he was put in jail for it. His captors put him on a ship to Rome to stand before Caesar, the king. But a strong wind came and carried the ship away from shore. The storm was blowing so hard that the men had to throw cargo overboard. They even had to throw out the ship's equipment!

"For many days, the men couldn't see the sun or the stars. They began to lose hope. But Paul told them to cheer up, that none of them would die. He told them that an angel had appeared to him in the night and told him, 'Paul, do not be afraid! I will save the lives of all those men sailing with you. So be cheerful and trust in God.' And that is what they did! They returned safely."

Lora was amazed! The Bible story helped take her mind off of the wind blowing outside the window.

God even has power over storms. He has wonderful power!

Your Turn

Aunt Carol and Lora saw God's power in the storm. Where do you see God's power?

_____

_____

Prayer

Dear God, your power is wonderful. Remind me that you are with me even when I'm afraid. Please protect me and guard me just as you did Paul. Amen.

Weather Wheel

What kind of weather did Paul face in the story? What is your favorite kind of weather? Draw a sun in one section, rain in another, clouds in another and a tree bending in the wind in the last section. We can see God's wonderful power in the weather.

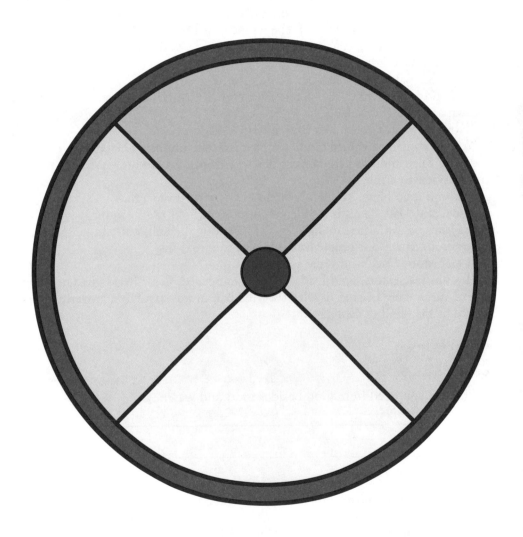

A Powerful Well

My God satisfies me.

Let anyone who is thirsty come to me and drink.

~ John 7:37

Happiness I Need

One evening, Lizzy's dad was helping her study for a spelling test.

"Desert. D-E-S-E-R-T. Desert," she repeated as Dad looked at the list.

Dad smiled. "I think you're ready for your test," he said. "But talking about the word 'desert' makes me thirsty."

"Me, too!" said Lizzy. "Let's get a cold drink."

Dad and Lizzy went to the kitchen and poured two glasses of soda. Then they sat down at the kitchen table.

"Now, let me tell you a desert story," said Dad.

"A man named Moses led God's people on a long journey. They had to cross a big desert. Their mouths became very dry and thirsty. So God told Moses, 'I will give you water to drink.'"

"I know," said Lizzy, "this is when Moses got water from a rock."

"No," said Dad. "This is a different story. God told Moses to dig a well. He showed him the spot where to dig. When Moses dug the well, water came spurting up like a fountain. God's people had enough water to drink!"

"Good story, Dad," said Lizzy.

"It's not just a story," said Dad. "It really happened. God always gives us what we need. Sometimes he gives us what we need before we ask. Only a powerful God can give us that kind of happiness."

Your Turn

1. What do you need from God besides food and water?

_____

_____

2. Did God ever give you something you needed before you asked? Tell about it.

_____

_____

Prayer

Dear God, thank you for your love and care. Come into my heart and give me what I need to satisfy me. Amen.

40

God's Spelling List

What do you need from God besides food and water? Make up your own list of "spelling words" that answer the question. Write your list on the spelling page below. Pray God will satisfy your needs.

Spelling List

1.

2.

3.

4.

5.

6.

7.

8.

Powerful Waters

God's power can help me.

God is…an ever-present help in trouble.

~ Psalm 46:1

High Waters

A little town rested along a winding river. A young girl named Torie lived with her family above the town's movie theater. Torie's father owned the theater. Torie worked at the popcorn counter on weekends, and her brother Mike sold tickets.

One summer, rain began to fall on the town. For many days and nights, the rains continued falling.

The movie theater was very popular because it was a place for people to escape the rain. One night, just after the movie started, the sheriff came to the theater. He wanted to talk to Torie's dad.

"A crack was found in the dam at the river," the sheriff told Dad. It was because of the heavy rains. "These rains had better stop soon or the whole town could be washed away with a flood. I'm telling you because we may need to remove the people from town tomorrow and bring some of them here to stay."

After the theater closed for the night, Dad turned on the TV.

"Let's watch the weather report," he said.

"More rain is in the forecast for tonight and tomorrow," said the weatherman.

Torie sighed. "Mom, Dad, what should we do?" she asked.

"My Sunday school teacher said, 'God is powerful and helps us when we are in trouble,'" said Mike. "Let's pray for God's help right now."

The family prayed. They asked God to show the strength of his helping power.

The next morning, Torie awoke to sunshine in her room. She ran to the window and looked out as the sun shone brightly.

"Mom, Dad, Mike!" she called. "God answered our prayers and saved our town. He is a powerful God! He does help in times of trouble!"

Your Turn

1. What kinds of help can God give?

_____

_____

2. When and how does God show his love?

_____

_____

Prayer

Dear God, I'm glad you can do anything and that You are powerful in my eyes. Thanks for answering my prayers. Amen.

Winding Problems

Write a problem on the winding river water. Pray for God's help. Remember, God always knows what's best. He may not answer in exactly the way you want, but he has a plan for your life and will do what is right for you.

A Powerful Guide

My powerful God will be my guide.

The LORD will guide you always.

~ Isaiah 58:11

The Tug

Julie and her sister lived near the ocean. Each summer they sat on the beach watching the tugboats.

The tugs pulled large ships called freighters out into the main waterway. These big ships couldn't steer themselves without a guide. The tug driver would sit high on his tug. He could see danger as the ship was pulled out.

Many people are like the freighters. They need someone to guide them.

In the Bible, we learn how God's people needed a guide, too. Leaving their homes in Egypt was scary, but the people of Israel had to get away from the mean prince of Egypt.

The people of Israel had little or no food, drink or clothing with them. God guided them by his goodness and care for them. A pillar of clouds led them in the daytime. The pillar shaded them from the sun as they traveled. When it stopped, they knew it was time to set up their camp. A fire led the way at night.

God was the perfect guide. Just like the tug went in front of the ship. God went in front of his people. God led them away from the dangers of the enemy.

God guided the people of Israel many years ago, but he still guides you today. God is a good guide because he can see danger before you do. Are you willing to follow him?

Your Turn

1. Why should you trust God?

_____

_____

2. How does God guide you today?

_____

_____

Prayer

Dear God, thank you for your loving guidance. Teach me to follow you. Keep me in your care always. Amen.

Behind a Powerful Tug

In each of the ship's portholes, draw the face of one of your family members. Ask God to guide your family as the tug guides this ship.

Girls for God

Jochebed

I will trust in God when I pray.

I call on the LORD in my distress, and he answers me.

~ Psalm 120:1

Not Always as They Seem

Kate got a teddy bear for her birthday. She was so happy! Kate named him "Patches" for the little patch of brown fur around one of his eyes.

One weekend Kate's family went on an out-of-town car trip to her grandma's. On the way, Kate's family stopped at a rest area for lunch. Kate sat Patches on a picnic bench while she and her brother tossed a ball around.

After the family ate lunch, they gathered their belongings to leave. Kate and her brother slipped into the backseat of the car. The family started out once again toward Grandma's house.

An hour later, Kate wanted to take a nap. She never napped without Patches. "Where's my bear?" she asked. "Oh, no, I don't have Patches!"

Kate had left Patches on the picnic bench at the rest area. She began to cry.

"Let's just pray and ask God to help us," said Dad.

"Things aren't always as they seem," Mom told her. "Do you remember Jochebed, Moses' mother? She thought her baby son was gone forever. She had to trust God when she placed him in the basket at the river. Then a princess found him and Jochebed was called on to be his nurse and caregiver. She was able to raise her son while he lived in the safety of the palace.

"So you see," said Mom, "we can trust God with Patches just as Jochebed trusted God with Moses."

Kate's dad called Grandma and told her they would be late. Then they turned back toward the rest area. After they parked, Kate jumped out of the car. She ran to the picnic table where they had lunch. There was Patches on the ground under the picnic table! She picked him up and hugged him.

"He's here! He's here!" Kate yelled.

"See, we can call on God and he will answer us," said Mom.

Your Turn

How can you trust God in a difficult situation?

_____

_____

Prayer

Dear God, show me how to trust in you even when things look difficult. Help me to learn to trust in your ways. Amen.

Patches & Prayer

Write the name of someone you trust on the bear's stomach. Pray and ask God to help you trust in him more than in the person whose name is on the bear's stomach. Trust God as Jochebed did!

Hannah

We can pray BIG prayers to God.

I know that you can do all things.

~ Job 42:2

Praying BIG Prayers

"That is the biggest elephant I have ever seen!"

"Look at the big hot air balloon in the sky!"

"What a big, strong arm my daddy has."

What looks big to you? Do you ever pray big prayers?

Sometimes your problems may seem too big for words. Big prayers call for big answers! God has big answers for your prayers. Many stories in the Bible tell of people who prayed big prayers. God answered them all in big ways. He will answer you in big ways when you pray big prayers.

A woman in the Bible named Hannah worshiped God in prayer and praise. So when she had a big problem, she knew where to go for big answers.

Hannah's big problem was that she wanted to have a child but so far she had no children. She told God if he would give her a child, she would raise the child to serve God.

God heard Hannah's big prayer and answered her in a big way. Samuel, a beautiful, strong son, was born to her. When Samuel was older, Hannah kept her promise to God. She took Samuel to the church to live with the pastor. Samuel learned more about serving and loving God.

When Samuel was grown, he became the father of King David. He was also a judge and a man who heard God's voice for the people.

Samuel wouldn't have been around to bless others if Hannah had not prayed big prayers. She trusted big prayers to produce big answers. Are you holding back from praying big prayers? Come on…be like Hannah and pray big prayers!

Your Turn

1. What big prayer do you want God to answer for you?

_____

_____

2. Does God answer every prayer the way you want?

_____

_____

Prayer

Thank you, God, for hearing my big and small prayers. I know you hear my prayers as you heard Hannah's. Amen.

My Big Prayer Page

Write a big prayer request on the page below. Remember that God will answer big prayers! Don't be afraid to ask for something big like Hannah did.

Anna

Pray without stopping.

Rejoice always; pray continually.

~ 1 Thessalonians 5:16-17

A Path of Prayer

Brett challenged his little sister, Amelia, to a bike ride. They rode down Deer Trail toward Crystal Lake. Deer Trail was known as the prettiest path in Fall City. Oak and maple trees hovered like giant umbrellas over the stones along the path. Curves and turns mysteriously appeared throughout the three-mile course.

Brett wondered if Amelia could ride to the end without stopping to rest. But Amelia was kind of a tomboy. She loved riding bikes and climbing trees alongside boys on her block.

Amelia surprised Brett by riding Deer Trail as far as "Old Mulberry." That old tree was known as the start of the "Mulberry Mile," the last mile on the trail. But by the time Brett and Amelia approached the last bump at the mulberry tree, Amelia couldn't go any farther. She had to stop and walk her bike.

"Don't stop, let's keep going," yelled Brett from up ahead. "Come on! Come on! Don't give up."

A woman in the Bible named Anna rode a trail of prayer. Unlike Amelia on Deer Trail, Anna never rested. Anna's husband died when she was a young woman and she never married again. Instead, she set out on a path of prayer. God led her to pray at the temple night and day.

Anna knew that praying made a difference in people's lives. So, for 60 years she prayed at the temple and didn't give up. She was one of the first people to tell others that Jesus is God's Son. If she had stopped praying, she may not have seen the blessing.

Can you pray without stopping? Can you pray even when there are bumps in your life? Can you pray each week without missing a day? Try going down the path of prayer!

Your Turn

Can you pray each day like Anna? When and how?

_____

_____

Prayer

Dear God, I am glad yYou love me and I can talk to You. Please give me the desire to pray for my family and others each day without stopping. Amen.

Deer Trail Prayers

Follow the prayers along the deer trail. Don't stop praying until you get to the end of the trail. Remember to be like Anna and pray each day.

Mary (Mother of Jesus)

God wants us to have special times with Jesus.

Mary treasured up all these things and
pondered [kept] them in her heart.

~ Luke 2:19

The Heart Bank

Do you have a great-grandma? (A great-grandma is your grandma's mother.)

Molly loved to visit her great-grandma. Molly listened closely as her great-grandma told amazing stories of the days before TV. Her great-grandma spoke of cars without seat belts, 25-cent movies and washing clothes in a tub of soapy water.

Molly imagined herself living back in those days. She thought how life would be different. Molly kept the things her great-grandma shared in her heart and mind. She stored them away. Molly thought about them often.

Mary, Jesus' mother, had many special thoughts she stored away, too. Her heart was filled with special times surrounding the birth of her Son, Jesus.

One story she remembered was when the shepherds came to Jesus' birthplace. They told her about angels appearing to them in the fields to tell that Jesus had been born.

When Mary heard this it made her happy. She remembered this special time with her baby. Memories of this event were stored in her heart and mind like money is stored in a bank.

Do you have special things stored in your heart and mind as Molly did? Do you remember any special times with Jesus as Mary did?

Your Turn

1. Tell about a special time you've had with Jesus.

_____

_____

2. Why do you think Jesus wants us to remember special times with him?

_____

_____

Prayer

Dear God, thank you for special times. Help me to remember special times with you and always keep them stored in my heart like a bank. Amen.

The Heart Bank

Think of a special time you have had with Jesus and draw a picture of it in the heart bank.

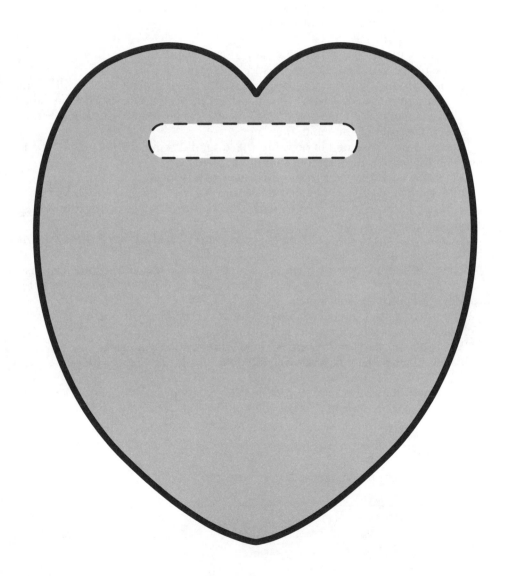

Esther

My prayers can reach to heaven.

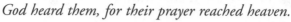

God heard them, for their prayer reached heaven.

~ 2 Chronicles 30:27

A Girl's Secret

"Maria, can you keep a secret?" asked Lauren.

"Sure!" Maria said. She really liked secrets. "What is it, what is it?"

"Promise you won't tell anyone?" checked Lauren.

"I promise! Now tell me!"

"Okay, my mom's going to have a baby," Lauren said softly.

Maria looked surprised. "That's great! I'll bet you can hardly wait."

A woman in the Bible, Esther, also had a secret. But her secret was very different from Maria's. Esther was a Jewish woman, which meant that she loved God. That was a problem because no one in the king's palace was Jewish. No one knew Esther was Jewish, not even her husband, the king.

Haman, who was second in power to the king, didn't like the Jews. So he made a law: "All the Jews in the kingdom should be killed."

When Queen Esther heard about the law, she was upset.

"Talk to the king about this," her uncle told her.

"I can't tell the king my secret," said Queen Esther. "If I go before the king without being asked, I'll be killed."

"Maybe God made you queen to save our people," said her uncle. "Maybe it is time to tell your secret."

"Okay," answered Queen Esther. "Bring together the Jews in the kingdom. Ask them to pray for me. Tell them to go without food or drink for three days. After three days, I'll go to the king. Then, if I die, I die."

After three days, Queen Esther went to the king. He held out his gold rod, which meant it was safe for Queen Esther to talk.

"What do you want, my queen? I'll give you whatever you wish," he said.

"Please change the rule that will kill my people, the Jews," Queen Esther pleaded.

The king listened. He made a rule keeping God's people safe. Esther's prayers saved a whole nation of people. What can you do with your prayers?

Your Turn

What do you want to change with your prayers?

_____

_____

Prayer

Dear God, thank you for answering my prayers. Thank you, God, for being with me all the time. Please let my prayers reach you in heaven. Amen.

Hands to Heaven

Think of something you can give up for three days to show God you are serious about your prayers to him. Maybe you could skip a favorite TV program or soda for three days. Write one thing you will give up on each of the three prayer hands below.

Dorcas

I can share my talent as I pray.

Be generous and willing to share.

~ 1 Timothy 6:18

Talents Shared with Prayer

Kara and her mother loved stitching as they prayed. They sewed clothes for the widows in their church. (A widow is a woman whose husband has died.) Sewing was a talent they used as they prayed for the widows.

Every stitch was a prayer for one of the women. As they sewed, they prayed: "Dear God, help this widow care for her child. Dear God, help this widow make enough money to feed her children. Dear God, help this widow be a good mom."

God was happy to use Kara and her mother as they prayed and worked. This was a mother and daughter who were generous and willing to share.

A woman in the Bible named Dorcas loved to sew as Kara and her mom did. Sewing was easy for her, and she was good with a needle and thread. She spent hours sewing clothes for widows.

Also, Dorcas loved God and wanted to show him by helping others. She used her time and talent for God's work.

God gave Dorcas a talent she could share with others as she prayed. God wants us to pray while using our talents, too. Is there a talent you have that can be shared with prayer?

Your Turn

1. What talent did Dorcas have?

_____

_____

2. How did she share her talent?

_____

_____

3. What talent do you have that could be shared with prayer?

_____

_____

Prayer

Dear God, I love you and want to use my talents. Show me the talents I have that can be used to help others. Also God, show me how to share my talent with prayer. Amen.

Share and Prayer Spools

On each spool, write a talent you have that you can use to help others. Talk with your parents about how you can use that talent with prayer.

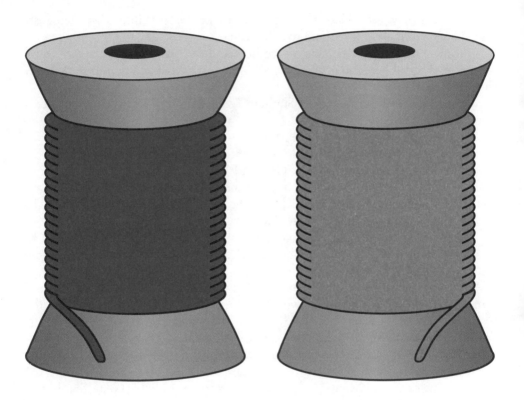

The Woman of Shunem

I will pray and serve others.

Our God is near us whenever we pray to Him.

~ Deuteronomy 4:7

Prayers Upstairs

Jennifer and her mom stood in the attic doorway. Mom pointed at the attic walls.

"When I pray, I feel God is telling me to make this attic into a bedroom," she said. "This will make a nice room for Grandma."

"Yeah," said Jennifer. "A table can go here and the bed over there."

Mom nodded her head in agreement. "We'll put a chair and a lamp stand here," she said.

"We sound like the woman of Shunem," said Jennifer. "I learned about her in Sunday school today."

"Tell me about her, Jenny," said Mom.

The two of them sat side-by-side on the attic steps as Jennifer relayed the story.

"The woman of Shunem knew God and I think she was a woman of prayer. You see, one day the prophet Elisha went to the woman's town. She asked Elisha to come for dinner. The woman was rich and she lived in a big house. While they ate dinner, the woman got an idea from God.

"'Elisha is a man of God,' she told her husband. 'So let's make a little room for him in our attic. Let's put out a bed and a table. Elisha can stay here when he comes to town.'

"So that's what they did. When Elisha saw the room, he was happy! It made him want to do something for the woman. The woman didn't have a child and that made her and her husband sad. So Elisha told the woman she would have a son by that time the next year. And the next year, the woman had a baby boy! The woman's home had been a place to serve God. So, God rewarded her with a son. God blessed the woman for following him."

"Good story!" said Mom. "Now let's get this room ready for Grandma. I know it will be a real blessing to have her here with us, too."

Your Turn

What could you do to help others?

_____

_____

Prayer

God, make me a girl who prays. Let me hear your voice and teach me to obey. Amen.

Prayer Room

Write a prayer below the picture of the room. Then go around your house and find a special place you can pray.

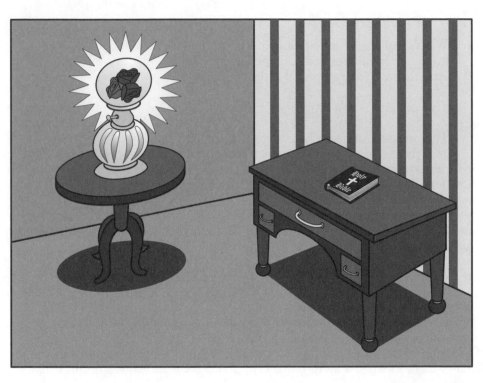

_____

_____

_____

_____

_____

Mary of Bethany (Part 1)

I can give something special to Jesus.

*A gift opens the way for the giver and ushers
the giver into the presence of the great.*

~ Proverbs 18:16

My Perfumed Gifts

"What's that smell?" asked Grace.

"It's the perfume your dad gave me for my birthday," said Mom.

Grace turned her nose upward and sniffed again. "Wow! It fills the whole room," she said.

"This perfume cost a lot of money," said Mom. "Dad spent his golfing money to buy it for me. He won't be able to play golf with his buddies for a whole month."

"That must mean he really loves you," said Grace, smiling.

Once there was a woman, Mary of Bethany, who filled a room with the smell of perfume as Grace's mother did. Mary was at a dinner party for Jesus. She wanted to show Jesus how much she loved him. The perfume she had was called "nard," and it cost a lot of money.

Mary bent down where Jesus was sitting. She slowly poured the perfume out onto his feet. It flowed over and between his toes. Then she wiped his feet with her hair. The sweet smell of perfume filled the room!

One of Jesus' helpers asked, "Why didn't Mary sell this perfume? Just think of the money we could have made to give to the poor!"

But, Jesus' friend didn't really care about the poor. He wanted to use the money for himself, and Jesus knew that.

"Leave Mary alone," said Jesus. "Mary is doing something beautiful for me. She saved the perfume for me. After I die, people will hear what Mary did tonight."

Jesus had done so much for Mary that she wanted to honor him in a special way. Mary's act of love cost a lot of money, but she knew Jesus was worth more than any perfume.

Your Turn

1. What did Jesus think about Mary's act?

_____

_____

2. What can you give to Jesus? What will it cost you?

_____

_____

Prayer

Lord, show me how I can give my love to you. Help me to love you more each day. Amen.

My Perfume Jar!

Do something special for Jesus. On the perfume jar below, write something you can give to him. It can be something you do or something you give away.

My Gift

Mary of Bethany (Part 2)

I will be close to Jesus.

"Who is he who will devote himself to be close to me?" declares the LORD.

~ Jeremiah 30:21

Close to Jesus

At family gatherings, Allison sat by her great aunt, Aunt Tilly. She often sat on the floor at Aunt Tilly's feet. Aunt Tilly was so kind and wise. Allison felt it was comforting to be with her.

But Aunt Tilly was old and sickly. Allison knew she wouldn't be alive much longer. She knew there would come a day when Aunt Tilly would go to heaven to be with Jesus.

"Let's go play," Allison's cousins would say. But Allison chose to stay with Aunt Tilly every time. Allison enjoyed hearing Aunt Tilly's stories and learning from her.

A woman in the Bible named Mary was like Allison, only she got to sit at Jesus' feet. One night, Jesus came to dinner at Mary's house. Mary and her sister, Martha, were happy to see Jesus. Martha hurried as she set the table and prepared the meal. She was very concerned about how the meal would taste. But Mary was content to sit listening quietly at Jesus' feet.

How wise and wonderful he is, Mary thought. Mary followed his every word.

Finally, Martha asked Jesus, "Don't you care that my sister isn't helping me? Tell her to help me!"

"Martha, Martha," said Jesus. "You shouldn't be upset and worried. Your sister has chosen to do the best thing."

Getting close to Jesus and obeying him are always the best things to do. Choose to be close to Jesus by reading the Bible and talking with him each day in prayer.

Your Turn

1. How can you tell Jesus that you love Him?

_____

_____

2. How can you find out what pleases Jesus?

_____

_____

Prayer

Dear Jesus, thank you for loving me. Teach me to please you. Help me to choose to be close to you by reading my Bible and talking to you in prayer. Amen.

Jesus and Me!

Draw yourself at Jesus' feet below. Think of ways to get close to Jesus!

The Sick Woman

I will look for Jesus and find Him.

You will seek me and find me when
you seek me with all your heart.

~ Jeremiah 29:13

Jesus Seekers

"Grab the edge of my shirt tail," Mom told Angie. "This is a big crowd and you could get lost."

Angie loved touching her mother. She felt safe holding onto her shirt. Angie also loved her mother's soft voice. She could always pick that voice out of a crowded room because it was very kind.

The Bible tells of a woman who picked Jesus out of a crowd. She had been sick for 12 years. Doctors tried to heal her, but couldn't. In fact, she was poor from giving all her money to the doctors.

The woman heard about Jesus. He came nearby and he moved into the center of a large crowd. So the woman twisted in and out through the crowd. She slowly pushed forward until she could see Jesus. Her hand reached out.

I just want to touch the hem on his clothes, she thought. *Then I'll be healed.*

Her hand touched Jesus. Right then, she was made well. From the top of her head to the tip of her toes, she was healed.

Jesus felt some of God's power go out of him. He looked around.

"Who touched Me?" He asked. Many people were pushing into him, but Jesus kept looking.

The woman finally came up to Jesus. She fell at his feet. Her body was shaking because she was so scared! Jesus listened as she told him everything.

"You believed, so you are well," said Jesus. "Now go home and be happy."

In the middle of a big crowd, a woman was able to find Jesus. When we look for Jesus we will find him and he will help us.

Your Turn

How can you find Jesus and get close to him?

_____

_____

Prayer

Dear Jesus, I'm glad that I can pray to you. When I pray I feel like I am close to you. Jesus, I want to stay close to you. Amen.

Finding Jesus!

Find Jesus in the crowd below and draw a circle around him. Try drawing yourself touching him.

The Best-dressed Girl

God's Special Clothes

I'll wear God's special clothes.

Be strong in the Lord and in his mighty power.
Put on the full armor of God.

~ Ephesians 6:10-11

Getting Dressed

"Hurry and get dressed. It's time for breakfast or you'll be late for school," Mom told Gina.

"What will I wear today?" said Gina as she jumped out of bed.

"Put on something warm," said Mom. "It's cold outside."

"Okay!" Gina thought for a minute. "I know, I'll buckle my belt around my waist. I'll put a vest over my shirt. I'll wear my hiking boots, too."

"Don't forget your jacket and hat," Mom said as she peeked into Gina's room.

Mom caught Gina standing in front of her floor-length mirror. Looking up and down at herself, she remembered one last item. "I almost forgot my Bible," she said to herself. "I'll carry it in my book bag."

"Come on, let's eat," said Mom. "Then I'll take you to school."

When you get dressed each morning, you put on your clothes as Gina did. But God wants you to put on another kind of special clothes. They are called "the armor of God."

The Bible says, "Be strong in God." That is what you do when you put on God's armor clothes. It means you are standing strong against Satan's plans. These pretend clothes help you fight against doing wrong things. God's clothes include a belt of truth and a breastplate of righteousness. They also include a helmet of salvation, a shield of faith and a sword of the Spirit, which is the Bible.

Telling the truth is like wearing a belt around you. Being kind to others is like wearing a breastplate over your chest. The Good News of peace is a pair of shoes worn on your feet to keep you ready. Believing Jesus is like holding a shield up in front of you. Wearing the helmet of salvation reminds you that Jesus died for you. Knowing God's Word is like carrying a sword for fighting.

Put on God's whole armor to fight bad ideas. Wearing God's armor will keep you close to God. God's special clothes protect you from evil.

Your Turn

What should you do when you're wearing the Good News of Peace?

_____

_____

Prayer

Lord God, keep me close to you. Help me to put on the whole armor of God to protect me from the enemy. Teach me to be strong in you and stand firm. Amen.

Armor Match

Read Ephesians 6:10-18 with your parents. Match each piece of God's armor to what it means.

belt of truth

breastplate of
righteousness

helmet of salvation

shield of faith

sword of the spirit

good news of peace

The answer is on page 238.

My Belt

I'll wear the belt of truth.

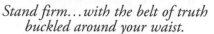

Stand firm...with the belt of truth
buckled around your waist.

~ Ephesians 6:14

A Belt of Truth

"Did you buckle your seat belt, Sara?" asked Dad.

"Yes! You know I always wear my seat belt, Daddy," said Sara.

"Good! A strong belt will keep you safe," he told her.

The Bible says to put on another kind of belt. The belt of truth! The Bible says, "Stand firm with the belt of truth buckled around your waist." God wants you to always tell the truth and do what is right.

Read the next two stories and decide which girl is wearing her belt of truth:

Suzie loved playing "Go Fish" with her younger sister, Megan. Suzie was the one who wrote down the scores. She cheated by adding numbers to her score. Megan never knew because she was too young to read numbers. Suzie usually won by changing the numbers in her favor.

While Kelly's mom was cooking dinner, she tiptoed into the kitchen.

"Can I have a cookie?" she meekly asked.

"No," said Mom. "It will spoil your dinner."

Kelly wanted to sneak back into the kitchen. But she knew that wouldn't be right since Mom had said no.

Which girl was wearing her belt of truth: Suzie or Kelly?

Suzie didn't have the belt of truth buckled around her waist. Being truthful is more than telling the truth. It is being honest and fair. Buckle your belt each morning. Being honest keeps you out of trouble, and it pleases God.

Your Turn

1. When should you wear the belt of truth?

_____

_____

2. What does a girl act like when she wears the belt of truth?

_____

_____

Prayer

Dear God, let me walk with the belt of truth buckled around my waist. Teach me to be real and to be honest. Help me to always tell the truth. Amen.

Buckle Up!

Wear the belt of truth below. Fill in the missing word on the buckle

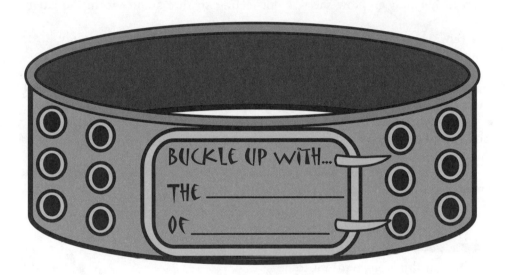

The answer is on page 238.

Truth or Blame?

I will be a girl of truth.

Each of you must put off falsehood and speak truthfully.

~ Ephesians 4:25

Blaming Others

"I think Amy stole my birthday money from my room," said Kylie.

Mom looked surprised. "Really? Are you sure?"

Mom had hired Amy to do some cleaning chores at their house. Mom trusted Amy, but Kylie looked convincing.

"The money was in my dresser drawer yesterday when Amy came to clean and now it's gone!" cried Kylie.

Suddenly, Kylie's stomach felt odd. She wasn't really sure the money had even been in her drawer. Now she was not feeling so sure about where she left her money.

But, Mom had believed Kylie right away. In fact, Mom was already on the phone talking with Amy's mom.

Kylie thought about how her lie might cause Amy to lose her job. Also, Amy may look bad in the eyes of others. "A little lie can cause a lot of hurt," she heard a quiet voice say. She knew it was God speaking to her heart and mind.

But Kylie's mother was wise. She talked to Amy before calling Amy's mother. She also asked Kylie to search her room for the money. Kylie found the money and Amy kept her cleaning job.

Lying can cause you and others many problems. Buckle your belt of truth around you. Then be strong in the Lord and don't lie!

Your Turn

1. Do you think Kylie meant to lie?

_____

_____

2. Can you think of a time when you lied and it hurt others? Share it with Jesus and ask him to forgive you.

_____

_____

Prayer

Dear God, I know you hate lies. Help me not to lie and to wear the belt of truth. Amen.

My Own Buckle

Make a belt of truth buckle for a pretend belt of truth! What would yours look like?

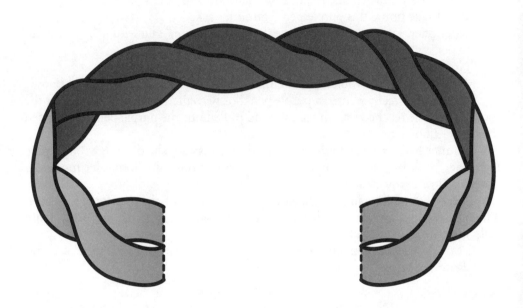

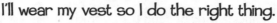

My Vest

I'll wear my vest so I do the right thing.

Stand firm…with the breastplate
of righteousness in place.

~ Ephesians 6:14

Doing Right

Summer went to work with her mother one day. She noticed colored pens in her mother's desk drawer. She reached her hand into the drawer.

"Can I take home this purple pen?" Summer asked.

"No, honey. I'm not allowed to take those pens home," said Mom. "But you can use the pens when you come to work with me."

"No one will know if I take just one," said Summer.

Mom frowned. "It wouldn't be the right thing to do. Besides, Jesus will know."

But Summer really wanted a purple pen. So she waited until her mother left the room. Then she reached into the drawer and pulled out the purple pen. She slipped it into her book bag.

Summer had a chance to do the right thing. Instead, she did the wrong thing. Later, her book bag fell over and the pen rolled out onto the floor. Her mom saw the pen. Summer was caught.

The Bible says, "Stand firm…with the breastplate of righteousness in place." The breastplate is a vest that helps us make right choices. It guards our hearts from evil. Summer didn't have her vest in place.

Let this song help you remember to wear your vest. Sing it to the tune of "Row, Row, Row Your Boat."

The Breastplate Song
Do, do, do what's right, do what's right today.
Always put your breastplate on,
nice and tight to stay.
Do, do, do what's right, do what's right today.
Always keep your breastplate on, close to your heart to stay.

Your Turn

How can wearing the special vest help you pick the right friends?

_____

_____

Prayer

Dear God, help me to wear the vest of doing the right thing. Teach me to make the right choices. Amen.

Vest Friends

Wearing the vest is important in making right choices. Write your friends' names on the vest below. Pray and ask God to give you friends who will help you stay close to him.

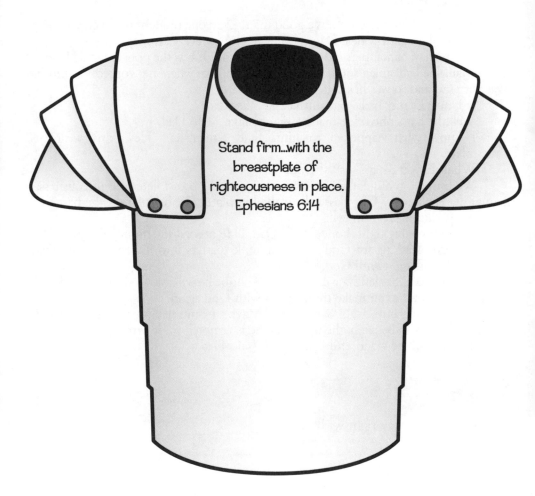

Stand firm...with the breastplate of righteousness in place. Ephesians 6:14

Being Ready

I will stay right with God.

No harm overtakes the righteous.

~ Proverbs 12:21

The Big Plate

Samantha's Uncle Danny was a good man. Everyone thought he loved God and wanted to follow him. Uncle Danny went to church every Sunday.

But one day, Samantha's father got a phone call. It was the police. Uncle Danny was in jail. He had stolen some money from the place where he worked. Samantha was very sad and so was her dad.

"Is Uncle Danny bad?" Samantha asked her dad.

"Well, he has sinned. He made a big mistake," said Dad.

"I know what happened to him," said Samantha. "He didn't wear his breastplate."

"What do you mean?" asked Dad.

"We learned in Sunday school about wearing the breastplate of righteousness," Samantha explained. "Our class calls it the big-plate. The big-plate is the part that helps keep your heart from evil."

"You're probably right, honey," said Dad. "He needed the money to pay off his bills. Instead of asking for God's help, he took matters into his own hands. That means he wasn't right with God."

Dad looked at Samantha with sad eyes. "I hope he will ask God to forgive him," Dad said. "Then he can make things right with God again."

"We can help him," said Samantha. "Maybe I can tell him about God's big-plate. Then he will be ready the next time he is tempted to do wrong."

"That would be wonderful, Samantha," said Dad.

Your Turn

1. How can you stay right with God?

_____

_____

2. How does the breastplate help you stay right with God?

_____

_____

Prayer

Dear God I want to belong to you. I want to be right with yyyyyou and stay right with you. Help me to wear my breastplate of doing right. Amen.

My Own Breastplate

Draw your own breastplate for doing right on the girl below. Write something on the breastplate that you did right this week.

People Peacemaker

I will wear the shoes of peace.

*Stand firm…with your feet fitted with the readiness
that comes from the gospel of peace.*

~ Ephesians 6:14-15

The Greatest Peacemaker

Colleen and her mother didn't get along well. They were always arguing. They argued over big things such as manners. They argued over little things such as clothes.

Mom would say, "Colleen, you need to wear a sweater. It's cold outside today."

Colleen would respond, "It's not cold, Mom, and I don't want to wear a sweater."

Colleen was not at peace with her mom. But her mom let her know how much she loved her. "Let's talk about how we can have peace with each other," Mom said. Colleen's mom was a peacemaker.

Madeline told her friend Lora bad things about Paige. Then Lora told Paige what Madeline said. Paige's feelings were hurt.

"We need to speak kindly to each other," said Lora. "We shouldn't talk about others behind their backs. Let's all be friends again." Lora was a peacemaker.

The greatest peacemaker is Jesus. Jesus died so we could be close to God and have peace with him. People who know Jesus today can fit their feet with shoes of peace.

Wherever you walk, you can have peace. Are your feet fitted with peace? Are you a peacemaker at school and home?

Your Turn

1. How do you think Jesus helps us make peace with others?

_____

_____

2. How can you be a peacemaker at school and home?

_____

_____

Prayer

Dear God, so many people are mean and they fight. Help me to make peace wherever I walk. Help me to tell others about the peace they can have by knowing Jesus. Amen.

Family Shoes

Write the names of your family members on the shoes below. Pray for each family member and ask God to give his or her feet the shoes of peace.

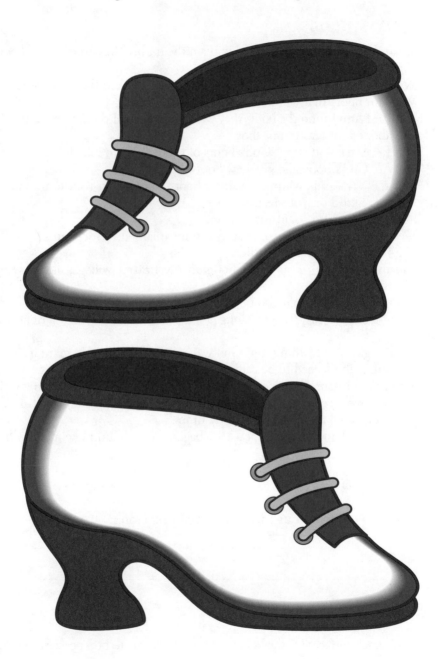

My Boots of Peace

I'll wear the boots of peace.

Be at peace with each other.

~ Mark 9:50

My Heart Boots

Ann and her parents were going hiking in the mountains. So Ann and her mom went shopping for hiking boots.

"What kind of hiking boots are you looking for?" asked the store clerk.

"We want boots that will be comfortable, but strong," Mom told the clerk.

Mom and Ann found the boots they wanted. In the car on the way home, Mom told Ann about another kind of shoe.

"Did I ever tell you about God's boots of peace?" Mom asked.

"No! Are God's boots like my new boots?" Ann asked.

"In some ways," said Mom. "But these boots you wear in your heart and mind. They aren't the kind on your feet."

"I don't understand," said Ann.

"Well, these are the boots of peace," Mom explained. "God wants us to live in peace with friends, parents and others."

"You mean when I wear God's boots in my heart I will get along well with friends?" asked Ann.

"Yes," said Mom. "You'll also be at peace with your brother and sister."

"It's not always easy to get along with people," said Ann. "Friends aren't always nice."

"That's right," said Mom. "But God wants us to be strong in getting along."

"Are you saying I need to be called a peacemaker?" asked Ann.

Mom hugged Ann. "Yes, 'peacemaker' is a good name for those who love Jesus. The more you wear your boots of peace, the more comfortable they'll feel. They will last forever and hold up in sad and happy times."

"Wow!" said Ann. "Boots of peace are beginning to sound like my new boots."

Your Turn

What should you do if your friends aren't getting along?

_____

_____

Prayer

Dear God, teach me to wear the boots of peace. Help me to be a peacemaker. Amen.

My Boots

Draw boots on the girl below. Then write on the lines names of people with whom you want to make peace or keep peace.

_____

_____

_____

_____

My Shield of Faith

I will carry a shield of faith.

Take up the shield of faith, with which you can extinguish all the flaming arrows of the evil one.

~ Ephesians 6:16

Stopping Arrows

Carrie was very poor. Her parents couldn't afford new clothes for her. One day at school some girls made fun of Carrie's shirt. Carrie's mom had bought it at a thrift shop.

"Look at that shirt," they said. "That's ugly!"

But Carrie knew Jesus loved her. She knew he didn't care what kind of shirt she wore. So instead of getting hurt or mad, she prayed, "Jesus, forgive those girls. They don't know you."

Carrie strongly believed in Jesus. Her belief was like a shield around her. God's Word was always a help to her.

Carrie used her faith like a shield. In Bible times men at war held shields in front of them. The shields protected against the enemy's arrows.

Put up a pretend shield to keep arrows from hitting your heart. Hold out your shield and fight the arrows!

Your Turn

1. How did Carrie keep from getting her feelings hurt?

_____

_____

2. What arrows come toward you?

_____

_____

3. How do you think God's shield can help you?

_____

_____

Prayer

Dear God, thank you for being my shield. Keep the arrows away from me. Thank you, God, for loving me and for caring for me. You are my shield. Amen.

Girls with Shields

On the shield of faith below, use the clues and write the names of women in the Bible who showed they carried their shields of faith.

Clues

1. Her husband died. She left her mother and father to live with her mother-in-law, Naomi.
2. She prayed for a child and God gave her a baby boy. She named him Samuel.
3. She hid spies on her roof.
4. She placed her baby boy in a basket and put him in the river to keep him safe.
5. She was very old. She was there when Mary and Joseph blessed their baby Jesus at the temple.

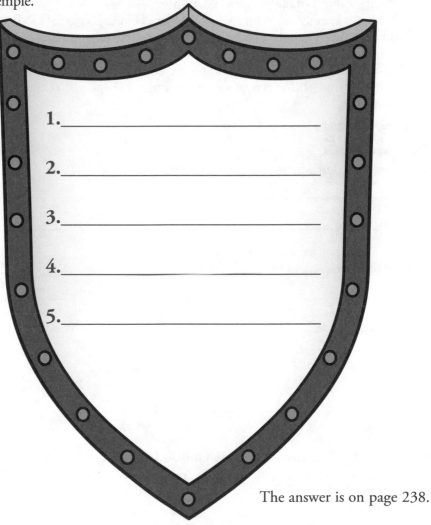

1. _____

2. _____

3. _____

4. _____

5. _____

The answer is on page 238.

More Faith

I will show others my faith.

I will show you my faith by my deeds.

~ James 2:18

Show Me

Charlotte and her older brother were watching TV. A girl in the show wanted to pick a fight with another girl. It wasn't over anything very important, but she still wanted to fight.

"Wow, they shouldn't fight," said Charlotte. "Especially over something so silly."

"Fighting isn't a good way to show your faith in Jesus, either," said Tommy. "They need to hold up their shields of faith in front of them."

"What's a shield of faith?" asked Charlotte.

Charlotte's brother rolled his eyes. "I told you before. It's part of God's armor for us," said Tommy. "The shield keeps belief in Jesus close to your heart and sin out."

"I want to wear the shield of faith," said Charlotte.

"Good!" said her brother. He clicked the control to turn up the sound on the TV. "Now let's watch the rest of the show and see if the girl changes her mind about fighting."

Your Turn

1. What is a good way to show someone you love Jesus?

_____

_____

2. How does the shield of faith help you?

_____

_____

3. What does it mean to be a Christian?

_____

_____

Prayer

Dear Lord, I believe that you are my God and Savior. Forgive me for not always showing that I believe in you. Help me to show my faith in you. I will put on the shield of faith. Amen.

My Own Shield

Color your shield of faith. Write on the shield something in which or someone in whom you have faith.

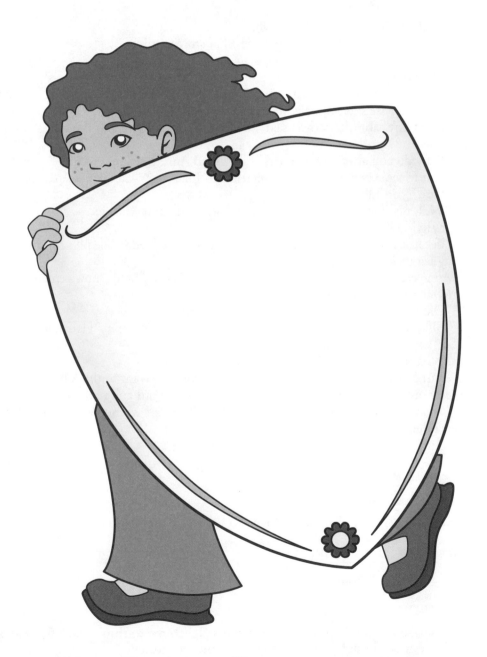

My Helmet of Salvation

I will wear a helmet of salvation.

Take the helmet of salvation.

~ Ephesians 6:17

A Different Hat

"Look at these cool hats," said Ellie.

Ellie and Aunt Maggie stood outside a hat store window.

"I like the green one," said Aunt Maggie.

"I like the pink one," said Ellie.

Aunt Maggie was a silly aunt in the eyes of Ellie's family. They called her the "hat lady" because she wore big, funny hats.

Ellie didn't care what others said. She loved Aunt Maggie and thought she was awesome.

"Why do you always wear a hat?" Ellie asked Aunt Maggie.

Aunt Maggie bent over and whispered into Ellie's ear. "Can you keep a secret?"

"Sure!" said Ellie.

"Well, my doctor said I should wear a hat," said Aunt Maggie.

"Why?" Ellie asked.

"Because my hair is falling out," Aunt Maggie explained. "The pills for the rash on my leg make my hair fall out."

Aunt Maggie covered Ellie's mouth with her finger. "Shhh, now remember, I don't want anyone to know."

"Okay!" said Ellie. "I'm glad it's nothing scary."

"I like wearing a hat for another reason," said Aunt Maggie. "Hats remind me of God's special hat, the helmet of salvation."

"What's God's helmet like?" asked Ellie.

Aunt Maggie smiled. "It's a pretend hat for when we want to think like Jesus. It protects our thoughts. The helmet lets us hear God's Word and remember it."

"Okay, I will wear my helmet of salvation. But can we buy a real hat, too?" asked Ellie.

"Sure! Let's go into the store!" said Aunt Maggie.

Your Turn

What thoughts do you have that need to be under the helmet of salvation?

_____

_____

Prayer

Dear God, teach me to protect my thoughts. Teach me to think like Jesus. Help me think good thoughts about people around me. Amen.

Hat Board Game

Use a bean or penny to play the game below with a friend. Roll a die to see how many spaces you should move.

A Steady Mind

I will keep my thoughts on Jesus.

The LORD knows all human plans.

~ Psalm 94:11

My Thinking Cap

"Put on your thinking cap," said Megan's teacher.

Megan stood at the chalkboard and held the chalk tightly in her hand. Forty-two plus 25 was the last thing on her mind! Instead, Megan kept thinking about how mad she was at Sarah. Earlier that day at recess, Sarah wouldn't jump rope with her. Instead, she played hopscotch with Betsy. Sarah was her best friend and they always played together at recess. Megan wanted to get back at her in the worst way.

Megan's thinking cap was on all right, but she was thinking the wrong things!

Megan's mom picked her up at school later that day.

"Why the sad face?" Mom asked.

"Oh, I keep thinking about something that happened at recess today," said Megan.

"What was that?" Mom asked.

"I want to get back at Sarah," Megan said. "I'll never forgive her!"

"Wow," said Mom. "I don't think it matters what she did. We need to talk about your bad thinking. It sounds like you have forgotten to wear your helmet of salvation today."

Megan squirmed in her seat as Mom talked. "Wearing the helmet of salvation can help you think like Jesus."

"Are you talking about a real helmet?" asked Megan.

"No," said Mom. "It's a pretend helmet of God's armor to protect your thoughts. It helps us think the way God wants us to think."

"You mean like being kind and forgiving?"

"Right!" said Mom as she pulled into the driveway. "The Bible says, 'The Lord knows the thoughts of man.' So God knows when we have unkind thoughts and hold anger for someone."

"I guess that means I should wear my thinking cap for God," said Megan. "And that means thinking the best about my friends and being ready to forgive."

"You got it!" said Mom.

Your Turn

How will you know when you are wearing the helmet of salvation?

_____

_____

Prayer

Dear Lord, I am sorry for not wearing the helmet of salvation. Teach me to put it on my head and think like Jesus. Amen.

A Good Thinking Cap

On the thinking cap below, write or draw a picture of what Jesus would want you to think when you are wearing the helmet of salvation. Look up Philippians 4:8 in the Bible for help.

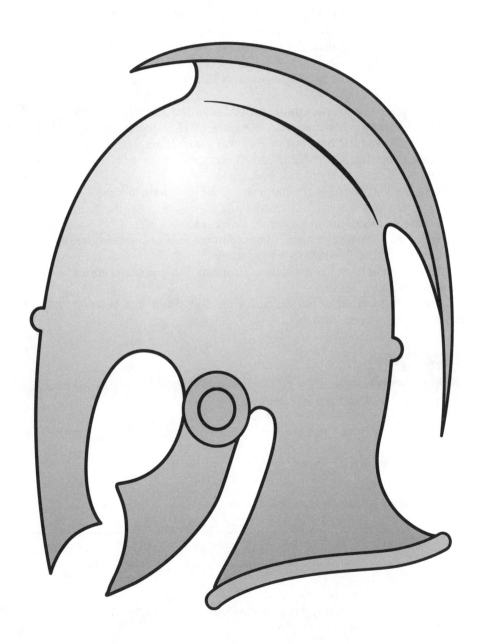

Fighting Evil

I will take up the sword of the Spirit.

Take…the sword of the spirit, which is the word of God.

~ Ephesians 6:17

The Sword

Tracy and Mary were playing dolls in the den at Mary's house.

"Let's play dress-up with our dolls," said Mary.

But just as they got their dolls dressed, in ran Mary's little brother, Timmy, with his friend carrying two swords and yelling, "This is war!"

"Put your swords away before you hurt someone," said Tracy. "Besides, you're stepping on our doll clothes."

"We're playing with the armor of God," shouted Timmy. "I must fight evil."

"Mom! Timmy is bothering us," yelled Mary. "He's stepping on our doll clothes."

"I'll try to keep the boys out of your way," said Mom.

"What's your brother playing?" asked Tracy.

"Oh, it's 'The Armor of God,'" Mary told her.

Mom stuck her head in the room where the girls were talking. "They're playing with the sword of the spirit," Mom told Tracy.

"What's so special about a sword?" asked Tracy.

"Well," said mom, "the sword of the spirit is the Word of God. It's part of God's armor. It protects us from doing wrong things."

Mary brushed back her doll's hair. "Learning Bible verses keeps us from getting into trouble. Right, Mom?"

"Right!" said Mom. "Remember, girls, the Bible is a weapon against sin. Learning it protects us from evil."

Your Turn

1. How can the Word of God help you?

_____

_____

2. Give a good reason to learn a Bible verse.

_____

_____

Prayer

Dear God, thank you for giving your words to me. Help me to use the sword to fight against doing wrong. Amen.

Between the Swords Quiz

Draw a line from the question to the matching answer between the swords.

How many books are in the Bible?	Psalms
Hide God's word in your_____.	The Gospels
How many books are in the New Testament?	66
King David wrote the book of_____.	27
Matthew, Mark, Luke and John are called?	heart

The answer is on page 238.

Sharpened Words

God's Word is a help to me.

The word of God is living and active.
Sharper than any double-edged sword.

~ Hebrews 4:12

The Loveable Facts

"Two plus one is three and two plus two is four."

"Two times two is four and two times three is six."

You can learn your math facts in school by saying them repeatedly. Writing down the facts can also help you remember them. You need to know math to keep score in games, to count money and for many other important things. Learning math is very important!

But Bible facts are more important. A girl named Alexis learned just how important Bible facts can be.

Alexis was very sad because a car had hit her dog. Alexis missed Muffy.

"I will miss Muffy sleeping at the foot of my bed at night," she cried.

Dad hugged Alexis as he tucked her into bed. "You know, the Bible says in 2 Corinthians 1:3, 'The God of all comfort, comforts us in all our troubles.' That's a good verse to know and learn. God wants to comfort you right now."

Dad's words made Alexis feel better. "It helps me to know God cares about Muffy and me," said Alexis.

"The Bible can change lives," said Dad. "God's Word can be a great help to us."

"I already feel better about Muffy," said Alexis as she snuggled into her bed.

Your Turn

1. What are some good ways to learn Bible facts?

_____

_____

2. How can you help others learn Bible facts?

_____

_____

Prayer

Dear God, thank you for the facts of your word. The best fact is that you love me and want me to be yours. Teach me to love your word and never forget it. Let me use your word to help others. Amen.

Loveable Words

Write below something you have heard or read in the Bible that you like. It can be a person, story or something you've learned such as "God loves me."

Loveable Words Page

My Guy Jesus

Jesus, My Safety

I feel safe knowing Jesus.

It's better to take refuge in the LORD than to trust humans.

~ Psalm 118:8

Titanic Trust

The "Titanic" was the largest ship of its day. It was considered to be unsinkable and people trusted its safety. But on its first journey from England to the United States, while people on board were eating, dancing and sleeping, the Titanic struck an iceberg. This supposedly unsinkable ship sank within 2.5 hours. Because the builders believed the Titanic could never sink, there weren't enough lifeboats. About 2,200 people died in the icy waters.

The Challenger and Columbia space shuttles exploded in the air. The Challenger blew up within seconds after lifting off. The Columbia exploded within seconds of entering the earth's air. Every crewmember from both shuttles was killed even though people had trusted those who made the shuttles.

In both situations, the most advanced manmade travel turned into failure. But Jesus' friends learned to put their trust in him rather than people. Crossing the lake in a boat, a large storm surprised Jesus and his friends. When the storm blew around them, waves crashed the boat. Jesus slept while his friends worried. They were so afraid that they woke him. Jesus stood and spoke to the storm.

"Be still," He said.

The winds died down and everything was still again. They learned it's better to trust in Jesus than in people.

Do you trust Jesus? You need to trust him. The only way you will truly feel safe is to trust in his care and protection.

Your Turn

1. How can Jesus help you feel safe?

_____

_____

2. Has there been any time recently when you have not felt safe? Whom were you trusting at that time?

_____

_____

Prayer

Dear Jesus, help me know you and your ways. Teach me to trust in you and not just what people can do. Help me to tell everyone that you can keep them safe, too. Amen.

A Safe Ride

Draw a picture of your friends in the boat with Jesus.

Jesus Is Here

I want to know Jesus is here.

Set me in your presence forever.

~ Psalm 41:12

Surprise Me

"Surprise!" said Abby as she jumped out from behind the sofa. Abby stood smiling in front of her mom. She pulled a little red box from behind her back.

"Mom, I wanted to surprise you on your birthday."

"Oh, Abby!" said Mom. "You did surprise me! Hey, Abby, did you know Jesus once surprised some friends?"

"Tell me about it," said Abby.

As Mom opened the red box, she told Abby a Bible story:

"One night Peter and his friends were fishing on the lake. They fished all night, but didn't catch anything.

Morning came and a man on shore called out to them. 'Don't you have any fish, my friends?'

'No,' they shouted back.

'Throw your net into the water on the right,' said the man.

They did just as the man said. Soon their net was so heavy they couldn't lift it! When they got to shore, a campfire was burning. The men were very surprised to see Jesus there. He had been the man calling from shore the whole time.

'Have some breakfast!' said Jesus."

"Jesus can surprise you, too, Abby," smiled Mom. "Jesus is near even when you're not looking for him. He wants to be near us all the time."

"Wow!" said Abby. "I want Jesus to surprise me."

Your Turn

1. How could Jesus surprise you?

_____

_____

2. Where are some places Jesus could surprise you?

_____

_____

Prayer

Thank you, Jesus, for being near me. Being near you makes me happy. Please surprise me, Jesus! Help me to think of you when I'm at school or play. Amen.

Breakfast with Jesus

Write on the breakfast fire below some places you go each week (for example, piano lessons, dance class, etc.). Think of how Jesus can surprise you there. Draw yourself having breakfast with Jesus.

Jesus Knows!

I'm glad Jesus knows everything.

[Peter] said, "Lord, you know all things."

~ John 21:17

Know-sy Jesus!

Casey was very angry with her father because at family meals he corrected her bad table manners.

I'm mad at Dad. I wish I had a different family, she thought.

Casey's family didn't know what she was thinking, but Jesus knew. Jesus knows everything you think and he sees what you do. He knows the good and bad things you say. Jesus is "know-sy" in a good way. That's because he loves you. Jesus knows the bad things you do and still loves you!

"Noel, time for bed," said Mom.

"Oh…I don't want to go to bed yet," Noel said. "Can I have a bedtime snack first? Please?"

"You had a chance to eat at dinnertime, Noel. Now its bedtime! Get your pajamas on, brush your teeth and get into bed," said Mom.

Noel was still thinking out how she could get a snack. "Okay, Mom!" she called from her bedroom.

But Noel didn't go to the bathroom to brush her teeth. Instead, she tiptoed into the kitchen. She put her hand inside the cookie jar and pulled out a hand full of cookies. Looking over her shoulder, she made her way to her bedroom. She quickly stashed the cookies under her bed covers.

Even though Noel's mom didn't catch her sneaking cookies, know-sy Jesus saw what she was doing. Noel was not doing the right thing. Jesus sees the good and bad things everyone does.

Jesus' friend Peter said, "Lord, you know everything." Jesus is so wonderful that He knows everything. But Jesus is always ready to forgive you. You can be glad Jesus is know-sy for you–in a good way!

Your Turn

Why should you be glad that Jesus is know-sy?

_____

_____

Prayer

Lord, please help me to think and act the way you want me to. I am glad you know everything. Jesus, help me to do the right things and obey my parents and teachers. Amen.

Know-sy Puzzle

Solve the puzzle on the lines above the girl's head.

1	2	3	4	5	6	7	8	9	10	11	12	13	14	15	16	17	18	19	20	21	22	23	24	25	26
A	B	C	D	E	F	G	H	I	J	K	L	M	N	O	P	Q	R	S	T	U	V	W	X	Y	Z

___ ___ ___ ___ ,   ___ ___ ___   ___ ___ ___ ___   ___ ___ ___   ___ ___ ___ ___ ___ ___ ___

12 15 18 4   25 15 21   11 14 15 23   1 12 12   20 8 9 14 7 19

– John 21:17

The answer is on page 238.

The Server Jesus

Jesus wants me to serve others.

*"Truly I tell you, whatever you did for one of the
least of these brothers and sisters of mine, you did for me."*

~ Matthew 25:40

A Big Helper

"You are a great helper, Amanda," said Mom.

Amanda poured the flour into a mixing bowl. "What can I do next?" she asked.

"You can help me stir the batter," Mom replied.

Amanda smiled, "I love being your helper, Mom."

"Amanda, you also please God when you help others," said Mom. "Helping others is serving Jesus. What else can you do in our family to help and serve others?"

"Well, maybe I can help you fold the clean clothes or set the table for dinner," said Amanda. "I know what else, I can help baby Josh put his toys away."

"Those are all good things, Amanda," said Mom as she gave her a big hug. "Serving is looking for opportunities to help someone. You are already a big help to Jesus."

The Bible says you should be like Jesus. Jesus said that the way to become great is to serve others. Jesus came to serve, not to be served.

Your Turn

1. How was Amanda a good helper?

_____

_____

2. How is Jesus your helper?

_____

_____

3. How can you help at home?

_____

_____

Prayer

Dear Jesus, thank You for dying on the cross to serve me. Help me to love others and serve them. Amen.

Mix and Serve

In the mixing bowl, write your plans to serve someone. After you serve each person, put a line through his or her name.

1. _____
2. _____
3. _____
4. _____

Jesus = Mercy

Jesus shows His mercy to me.

With the LORD is…full redemption.

~ Psalm 130:7

Giant Mercy

Jenna's dog, Fluffy, kept getting lost. Fluffy was a big dog and could easily jump the backyard fence. One day, Fluffy got away and was lost for three days.

"Dad, why does Fluffy keep jumping the fence?" Jenna asked.

"I guess he doesn't realize how much he needs our help," said Dad. "When he gets cold and hungry he will find his way home."

Mom frowned. "I'm not so sure I even want that mangy dog back again. He has run away for the last time!"

Dad gave mom a sad look. "Now, honey," he said. "Show some kindness and mercy toward Fluffy."

"Please, please, Mom!" begged Jenna.

Dad pulled the phone book from the drawer. He planned to call the animal shelter to ask if Fluffy had been picked up. The dogcatcher often found lost dogs.

"What's 'mercy' anyway?" Jenna asked.

"Mercy is showing kindness and love to someone. Even when the person may not deserve it," said Dad.

"Oh, I know! Like when I used Mom's best china bowl for a mud pie and broke it. I thought I would be grounded my whole life. But, you showed mercy and grounded me three days instead," said Jenna.

"That's right," said Dad, "You see, like Fluffy, people want to do what they want to do. But Jesus died so everyone could have forgiveness for going his or her own way. With Jesus there is giant mercy."

"Wow! That is great and wonderful," said Jenna. "For Fluffy's sake, I'm sure glad you know about mercy."

Your Turn

Why does Jesus want to give mercy to you?

_____

_____

Prayer

Dear Jesus, thank you for the mercy you give me. Help me to show mercy to others. Amen.

Mercy Fence Puzzle

Use the numbers below to solve the puzzle on the fence. Uncover what Jesus wants to give us.

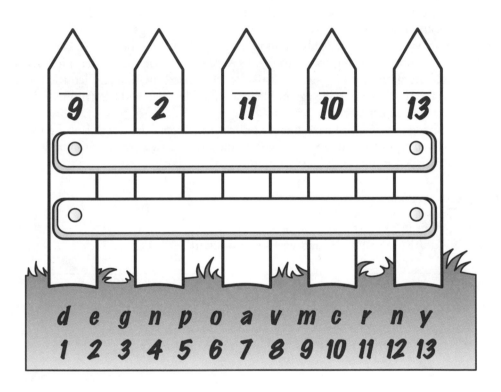

$\overline{9}$ $\overline{2}$ $\overline{11}$ $\overline{10}$ $\overline{13}$

d	e	g	n	p	o	a	v	m	c	r	n	y
1	2	3	4	5	6	7	8	9	10	11	12	13

The answer is on page 238.

Wonderful Jesus!

Jesus does wonderful things.

Remember the wonders he has done.

~ Psalm 105:5

A Report on Jesus

"My dad is wonderful because…he can hit the ball over the fence," Kate wrote in a school report about the most wonderful person she knew. In her mind, Kate's dad was by far the strongest and best. He could fix her bike, paint her toy shelf and put the wheel back on her scooter. He could even do all those things in one day.

Kate knew she would never forget the wonderful things about her dad. She decided he was worth writing about and reporting about in school.

Jesus is worth reporting about, too! Jesus is mighty, which means that He can do anything. The Bible tells of Jesus' great works. He healed the sick and fed the poor. He made the dead come to life again. He made the blind see and the crippled walk. Jesus even walked across the water!

Reporting memories of friends and family is important and good. But the Bible reminds us to report to others on our wonderful Jesus. Jesus wants you to remember his great works and he wants to show them to you today.

Your Turn

1. Why did Kate think her dad was so wonderful?

_____

_____

2. What are some wonderful things Jesus has done for you?

_____

_____

3. What do you think Jesus can do for you today?

_____

_____

Prayer

Dear Jesus, help me to remember what you have done in the past. Help me to trust you for what you can do today. Amen.

A Picture Report!

On the left side below, draw a picture of someone in your family doing something you want to remember about that person. On the right side, draw a picture of what you want to remember about Jesus.

My Report Page

In My Father's House

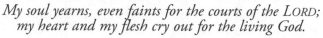

I want to be in God's House.

My soul yearns, even faints for the courts of the LORD;
my heart and my flesh cry out for the living God.

~ Psalm 84:2

Jesus and Me in God's House

"Christina, it's time for supper," called Mom.

"Christina isn't here, Mom. She's at the church," said her brother, Mike.

"Oh, that's right, I forgot she had play practice after school," said Mom.

"She's just about lived at church this week," Mike said.

"I guess you're right," said Mom. "Monday she had choir; Tuesday, prayer team; and tonight, play practice. I guess Christina wants to be as close to Jesus as she can."

Mom smiled at her son. "And, being in God's house makes her feel close to Him."

"You don't need to go to church to feel close to Jesus," said Mike.

"That's true," said Mom. "But if that's one way Christina feels close to Jesus, then that's okay. Christina always says, 'It's just Jesus and me when I'm at church.' Even Jesus liked being at church when as a boy," said Mom.

One time Jesus' family went to a special party in a town near Jerusalem. When the party was over, they started for home. Jesus stayed behind, but his parents didn't know where he was. They thought he was with their group.

Mary and Joseph traveled a long way before they noticed Jesus was missing. They looked among their friends and family, but didn't find him. Alarmed, they tracked back to town looking for him. They looked everywhere!

Finally, they found Jesus in the church. Jesus was sitting with the Bible teachers asking questions. Everyone was amazed at how much Jesus knew about God.

Mary asked, "Son, why have you done this to us? We were so worried."

Young Jesus replied, "Why do you look for Me? Didn't you know I'd be in my Father's house?"

Your Turn

Why did Jesus like to be in the church when he was a boy?

_____

_____

Prayer

Dear God, I want to be with you in your house. Give me a desire to go to church and learn more about you. Amen.

From Home to Church

Use a marker or crayon to follow the girl from her home to the church. Read what you can do when you get to church. Circle your favorite things, or pick something new you can do there.

The answer is on page 238.

Sunday Giving

Jesus wants me to give to Him on Sunday.

*The Sabbath was made for man,
not man for the Sabbath.*

~ Mark 2:27

My Giving Day

Erica watched the TV news one night just before Christmas. She heard a sad story about a little boy and his family. A cord to their Christmas tree had started a fire. The family's house burned to the ground. The boy had no toys and there was no money to buy Christmas presents. Now the family was staying in a shelter for homeless people.

After watching the news, Erica wanted to give to the family.

"I can use my allowance to buy the boy a Christmas toy," she told her parents.

Her parents agreed, but her family was so busy the only day they could visit the shelter would be Sunday.

"I'm not sure we can go to the shelter Sunday," said Mom. "We have church."

"Oh, I think we can find time on Sunday to take the gift," said Dad. "After all, Jesus gave out gifts on Sunday. We can, too."

"Did Jesus give away toys on Sunday?" asked Erica.

"No," said Dad. "He gave healing and food! One Sunday, Jesus healed a man whose hand was small and bent. He did it in front of the whole church so they would see that it is right to do good things on Sundays."

"Wow," sighed Erica. "I guess Jesus wants Sunday to be a day for giving."

Mom looked over at Dad as she put her arm around Erica. "It's good to give for Jesus on Sunday," she said.

Your Turn

1. Why did Jesus want to show people it is good to give on Sunday?

_____

_____

2. What do you give at church on Sundays?

_____

_____

Prayer

Dear God, help me find ways to give to others on Sunday and every day of the week. Amen.

My Giving Calendar

Write below something for each day of the week that you can give to someone in need. It doesn't need to be a material item (for example: a hug, make a meal or cookies for a neighbor, etc.) Circle the Sunday gift!

Monday
_____
_____
_____
_____
_____
_____

Thursday
_____
_____
_____
_____
_____
_____

Tuesday
_____
_____
_____
_____
_____
_____

Friday
_____
_____
_____
_____
_____
_____

Wednesday
_____
_____
_____
_____
_____
_____

Saturday

Sunday
_____
_____
_____
_____
_____

Exercise with Jesus

Jesus wants me to be strong for Him.

Train yourself to be godly.

~ 1 Timothy 4:7

Jesus Drills

Lexi loved gym class because Mr. Dell led the class in games. Each class began with fun exercise drills.

"Stretch, one…two…three…four. Touch your toes, and bend your knees," shouted Mr. Dell. "Now, run in place.

"Exercise drills make us strong," said Mr. Dell as he showed his arm muscles. "Exercise gives us energy and that's good for our bodies."

God gave you a body and it is important to God that you take care of it. Being strong helps you to fight off flu and colds.

Jesus was strong, but not necessarily from exercise. He was strong with the things of God. His drills were in prayer and reading God's Word each day. God wants you to exercise your body, your mind and your spirit.

You can exercise your spirit. Stretch by praying many short prayers several times a day. Reach for your Bible. Run to tell others about Jesus. Become strong for God by doing your Jesus drills!

Instead of showing your arm muscles, show your God muscles. Then everyone will see love, peace and the sweetness in you!

Your Turn

1. Should you exercise your body? Why?

_____

_____

2. What can you do to exercise your God muscles?

_____

_____

3. How will showing your God muscles help others?

_____

_____

Prayer

Help me not to be lazy in learning about you. Help me to be strong. Let me be a girl who does her Jesus drills each day! Amen.

Exercise for Jesus

Look at the girls below and think of a Jesus drill for each one that will help you grow strong in God. Finish coloring the girls and then perform your drills.

Jesus' Power!

Jesus did the powerful things God told him to do.

We told you about the coming of our Lord Jesus Christ in power.

~ 2 Peter 1:16

The Fish & Coin

Have you ever been to a fair? Amelia loved the fair, especially the fishing booth. Behind a curtain at the booth was a small pond. The booth worker gave Amelia a fishing pole. Amelia threw the fishing line over the curtain. Each time, she caught a token coin to buy a toy at the booth.

A man in the Bible also went fishing for money. He was in Capernaum. Jesus and his friends came to this fishing town. When the tax men saw Jesus and his friends, they wanted them to pay the church tax.

Jesus' friend Peter didn't think they should have to pay the tax. But Jesus said, "We don't want to make these tax men angry. So, go fish in the lake! Throw your line in as far as you can. When you catch a fish, open its mouth. Look inside and you will find money. Give that coin to the taxman."

Peter could see how powerful Jesus was. No man can make coins come from a fish's mouth!

Peter wanted to obey Jesus, so he did what Jesus asked. How wise and powerful Jesus is. Jesus did the powerful things God told Him to do.

Your Turn

1. Are you surprised that Jesus could put a coin in a fish's mouth?

_____

_____

2. Why do you think Jesus had Peter go fishing to get the coin? Why didn't he just give it to him?

_____

_____

3. What surprises you most about Jesus' power?

_____

_____

Prayer

Dear Jesus, thank you for your power and love. Help me obey you. Show me your power each day. Let me see your power at school, play and always. Amen.

Power Coins

Color the fish with coins that show a girl obeying Jesus (turn the book to see the picture better). Draw an X over the remaining coins.

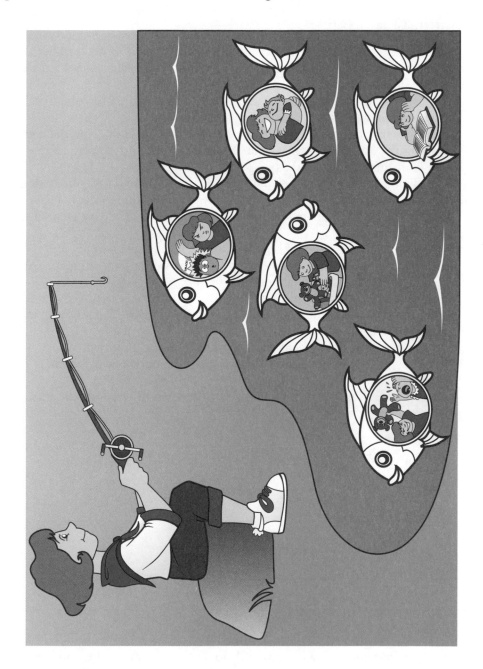

Jesus Followers

I will always follow Jesus.

Follow God's example.

~ Ephesians 5:1

I Follow the Leader

"Follow me!" said Miss Meyer, the second grade Sunday school teacher. The class loved "Follow the Leader." Since it was Christmas time, Miss Meyer led them around the Christmas tree.

Miss Meyer and the kids went in and out between chairs. Everyone marched out of the classroom and down the hallway and back again.

When they returned for a snack, Miss Meyer said to her class, "You did a great job following the leader. Christmas is an especially good time to play follow the leader. At Christmas, we honor the best leader: Jesus.

"The Bible says we should be followers of Jesus. I led you to places in our building that made it hard to follow. In the hallway, it was kind of dark. That's the way it is when we decide to follow Jesus. Sometimes life is hard and we aren't always sure where we are going."

"You mean following Jesus is like being in a dark hallway?" said Jamie.

Miss Meyer smiled. "No! Following your own way is like being in a dark hallway. Following Jesus is being led into the light."

Miss Meyer asked the class to come closer to her. "You see, Jesus is the light of the world," she said. "Following him leads us to the right places. We follow Jesus by doing the right things."

"Do you mean like loving God and our friends?" asked Shannon.

"That's right!" said Miss Meyer. "Don't forget about obeying teachers and parents, too."

Jesus is the best leader for every good thing. We need to be good followers.

Your Turn

1. What can you do to follow Jesus?

_____

_____

2. How is it difficult to follow Jesus?

_____

_____

Prayer

Dear Jesus, help me to follow you in all I do and say. I want to be a follower of you, but I don't always know how. Please teach me to be a good follower. Amen.

The Jesus Line

Follow your leader, Jesus. Draw yourself in the line behind Jesus. Also, draw your family members behind Jesus.

Open My Heart

Open the eyes of my heart, Lord.

For you were once darkness, but now you are light in the Lord.

~ Ephesians 5:8

The Blind Game

Rachel and Amanda loved to play "blind man." One girl tied a scarf over the other girl's eyes. Then the sighted girl led the blind one by the arm around chairs and tables. The girls wanted to feel what it is like to be blind.

"Be careful," Rachel's dad told the girls. "Don't bump into anything."

When they were done playing, he said, "Girls, 'blind man' is more than just a game. Some people have sight, but are blind."

"Really? What do you mean, Dad?" asked Rachel.

Dad explained that people see with their eyes but not with their hearts. "We don't always see the things of God. But Jesus wants to open the eyes of our heart so we can understand more about God's Word. Then we will feel what he feels and know his will."

The girls listened to what Rachel's dad was saying. "I want my heart's eyes to be open to Jesus," said Amanda.

"Me, too," said Rachel.

The Bible tells of a man who was born blind. As Jesus walked along, he came to the man.

"Why is this man blind?" Jesus' followers asked.

Jesus spat on the ground. He made mud from the dirt and put it on the man's eyes.

"Go," He said. "Wash off the mud."

The man washed the mud off his eyes and he could see Jesus for the first time. Soon he understood the things of God.

The man's eyes were open but the eyes of his heart were also open. Sometimes your heart is like the man's eyes. At first it is closed and blind. Then Jesus comes in and touches you. After that, you begin to understand the Bible and see things God's way. Jesus can make you the girl you should be. Open your heart's eyes today.

Your Turn

What can you do to make sure your heart's eyes are open?

_____

_____

Prayer

Dear Jesus, open the eyes of my heart so I can see you. Amen.

My Heart's Eyes

Use a crayon or marker to turn the blind heart into a seeing heart. Find the secret message at the bottom of the page. Write each letter using the key from below.

S	L	J	A	P	S	C	N	E	U	E	O	V
1	2	3	4	5	6	7	8	9	10	11	12	13

$\overline{}_{2}\ \overline{}_{12}\ \overline{}_{13}\ \overline{}_{9}\quad \overline{}_{3}\ \overline{}_{9}\ \overline{}_{6}\ \overline{}_{10}\ \overline{}_{6}.$

The answer is on page 239.

Obedient Jesus

I will obey for Jesus.

And this is love: that we walk in obedience.

~ 2 John 1:6

Show Me

Brittany usually obeyed her parents. She watched as her older sister, Ann, listened and obeyed. Ann did what her parents wanted. She did chores and homework without even being asked. Ann always did her best. She even prayed and read her Bible each day!

Brittany was glad to have an older sister to show her how to obey her parents and Jesus. But it was hard to live up to her!

"Thanks for showing me how to act, Ann," said Brittany. "You always do everything perfectly."

"I've always wanted to be a good example for you, little sis," said Ann. "But I'm not perfect. Guess who was the most perfect child who ever lived?"

"Tell me," said Brittany.

Ann picked her Bible up from the table. "It was Jesus," answered Ann as she flipped through the pages. "When Mary, his mother, told him to fill the water jugs, he did it at once. His father, Joseph, was a carpenter. He probably helped him saw and hammer wood. He didn't even think of disobeying."

"Do you think Jesus ever played?" asked Brittany.

"I'm sure He did," Ann said. "But, Brittany, he did the things God wants you and me to do. Like obey our parents and obey God in all we do and say."

If you love Jesus, you should want to obey your parents. Maybe you don't have someone like Ann to show you how to obey, but Jesus can show you from his word. Ask Jesus to make you more like him.

Your Turn

1. Why do you think Jesus wanted to obey his parents?

_____

_____

2. Can you ever be perfect as Jesus was?

_____

_____

Prayer

Dear Jesus, thank you for showing me how to obey. Help me to become more like you. Help me to obey my parents and teachers. Amen.

The Show Me Girls

How does Jesus show us how to obey? How can you show someone how to obey? Follow the directions below:

Jesus Shows Me

Write or draw here how Jesus shows you how to obey.

I Show Others

Write or draw here how you can show others how to obey.

Jesus the Word Keeper

Jesus keeps his word.

My words will never pass away.

~ Mark 13:31

Passing Words

Riley told Kristin, "Yes, I will trade you my pink headband for your silver belt." But Riley lost her headband and couldn't keep her word. So Riley's words passed away.

Kaitlyn told Molly, "I will come to your birthday party." But Kaitlyn caught the flu and could not go to the party. Her words passed away.

A storekeeper put an ad in the paper. The ad said, "Beautiful Dolls for Sale." But when Sarah went to buy her doll there were none left. The storekeeper couldn't keep his word. His words passed away.

Greta promised to go skating with her friend after school. "I promise I will meet you at the skating rink today," said Greta. But Greta's mother had made a dentist appointment for her that afternoon. Greta was unable to keep her promise to her friend. Her words passed away.

The words of people will pass away, but Jesus said, "My words will not pass away." Jesus keeps his word every time. His words are real and true!

Jesus said, "When you seek me, you will find me." We can trust Jesus to keep those words.

When Jesus says, "With God, all things are possible," it's true!

When Jesus says, "I will forgive you and save you," you can count on it!

Jesus is a word keeper. He will always keep his word to you. He also wants you to keep your word to others.

Your Turn

1. Tell about a time you couldn't keep your word.

_____

_____

2. Whose words do you think are stronger than any words?

_____

_____

Prayer

Dear Lord Jesus, I'm happy your words won't pass away. Thank you, Jesus, for keeping your word. Help me to keep your words in my mind and heart. Jesus, help me to keep my word to others. Amen.

The Word Keeper Puzzle

Unscramble the verses in each thought balloon below. Memorize them!

The answer is on page 239.

King Jesus

Jesus can be my King.

He is not here; he has risen.

~ Matthew 28:6

The King's Stone

Some women went to the stone tomb of a dear friend who died. Their dear friend was Jesus.

The women saw that Jesus' grave was open. To their surprise, two angels were there. One angel said, "Don't be afraid! I know you are looking for Jesus. He is not here! He has risen!" Then the women hurried to town to tell what they had seen.

Jesus had told people he is the Son of God. He had taught people how to be forgiven for doing wrong. Jesus told people He had come to save them from sin.

Jesus was followed everywhere. Old people, children, mothers and fathers followed him. Sick people came to him to be healed. When they felt his love, they wanted to praise him as King.

Evil rulers didn't love him. They put Jesus in jail. He was beaten and hung on a cross to die. But Jesus had great power. He could have stopped the evil men. Instead, he was willing to die so we could be forgiven.

Three days after Jesus died, something happened. Suddenly, the earth shook. An angel came down from heaven. The angel rolled away the stone at the door of his tomb. The soldiers on duty fell down as if they were dead. When they woke up, the angel and Jesus were gone!

Then the women came. Jesus' friends were full of happiness and praise that morning. It was the first Easter morning for our risen King. That's why we call him "King Jesus."

Your Turn

1. Why do you think the rulers killed Jesus?

_____

_____

2. Why do you think Jesus should be your King?

_____

_____

Prayer

Dear God, I praise you for that morning. Please show yourself in my life. Thank you, Jesus, for being my King. Amen.

My King's Stone

Think of some reasons why you should make Jesus your King. Write them on the stone below (turn the book to see the picture better).

Jesus Is Good

I see the goodness of Jesus everywhere.

Taste and see that the LORD is good.

~ Psalm 34:8

Taste and See...

"Would you like a piece of cake?" Mom asked Lily.

"Sure," said Lily. "But I want to taste a bit and see that it is good first."

"You just told me a Bible verse," said Mom.

"What?" asked Lily.

"You said 'taste and see if the cake is good.'"

"The Bible says, 'taste and see that the cake is good?'" Lily smiled as she washed down a bite of cake with a glass of milk.

"No," laughed Mom. "Taste and see that the Lord is good."

"I guess I did say a verse, didn't I? What does it mean, Mom?" Lily asked.

"Just what it says," Mom told her. "It means that Jesus our Lord is good and that the beautiful earth shows his goodness."

"Like green grass and blue sky?" asked Lily.

"Yes, but don't forget the sunshine each day and the moon at night. There's a lot of the Lord's goodness out there," said Mom. "All of creation shows the Lord's goodness and everything we have. Lily, remember the red bike you got for your birthday last year?"

"Sure," said Lily.

"That was the Lord's goodness. Your family, home, and friends are the Lord's goodness to you."

As Mom washed Lily's cake plate she said, "God's Word says to taste and see that Jesus is good. That means we should enjoy knowing him."

"Wow," said Lily. "Jesus is as good as a piece of cake."

"He is much better than that, honey." Mom placed her hand on Lily's head. "We can see Jesus in everything that is good. We can see that he is good."

Your Turn

What do you think it means to taste the goodness of Jesus?

_____

_____

Prayer

Dear Jesus, your goodness is all around me. Help me to see you in everything that is good. Amen.

Jesus Goodies

Draw three of your favorite sweets or treats below. Tell someone where you have seen the goodness of Jesus in your life.

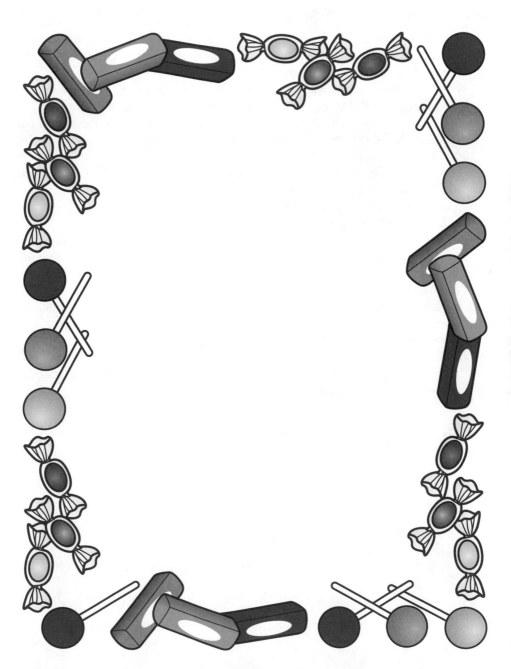

Best Friends

Jesus wants to be my friend.

I have called you friends.

~ John 15:15

On the Road Friends

Kylie first met her best friend, Kim, at camp. It was on the road to the camp store. Kim noticed that she and Kylie had on the same T-shirt: "Girls Rule!" Then they started talking.

Kylie's life was changed when she met Kim. Kim was fun to be with and she made Kylie laugh. Kylie felt happy inside when she and Kim were together. The two girls told each other everything. Kylie knew she had made a special friend in Kim.

A man in the Bible named Saul met a new friend on a road, too. Saul was riding a donkey headed for a town called Damascus. He was going to make trouble for the followers of Jesus. But, all of a sudden, a bright light came from heaven. It shone all around him and he fell to the ground.

"Saul, Saul, why do you hurt me and my people?" the voice called.

"Who are you?" asked Saul.

"I'm Jesus," said the voice. "I'm the one you are hurting. Get up! Go to Damascus."

Saul got up and opened his eyes. But he couldn't see anything! A man took his hand and led him into the city.

God had sent this man to pray for Saul. The man put his hands on Saul. Saul's hate for Jesus and his followers was turned into love. Then, a thin covering fell off Saul's eyes. He was happy that he could see again! But he was mostly happy that he met his new best friend, Jesus.

Saul was changed because he met Jesus on the road that day. Jesus became Saul's best friend. Saul talked to Jesus and told many people about Jesus' love. Knowing Jesus changed Saul. Jesus can change you, too.

Your Turn

How can Jesus change you?

_____

_____

Prayer

Show me ways I can meet you and love you. Help me to love others and be a good best friend. Amen.

The Camp Road

Draw a picture of you and your best friend on the road with Jesus.

Trusty Jesus

Jesus wants me to trust him.

Trust in the LORD and do good.

~ Psalm 37:3

Swimming In Trust

Erin read a bedtime Bible verse with her dad. It said, "Trust in the Lord and do good."

"What does 'trust in the Lord' mean?" she asked. Dad was Erin's Bible hero. He knew everything about the Bible.

"Do you remember your swimming lesson this morning?" asked Dad.

"Of course," said Erin. "I learned to dive into the water."

"Okay, how did you learn to dive?"

"I'll tell you and show you," explained Erin. "First, my teacher lifted me to the edge of the pool and told me to stretch out my arms. Then she said to put my arms together like a rocket ship and point toward the water. Then I had to point my head down and dive."

Dad smiled as he watched Erin act out her lesson. "What did you do next, Erin?"

"I dove in and swam to her," said Erin.

"How did you know she would be there after your dive?" asked Dad.

"I knew," she said. "I have learned to trust her when I swim. She would never let me drown."

"See, you trusted your teacher," said Dad. "You were sure she would catch you."

Erin was beginning to understand the meaning of the bedtime verse. "I think I know what this verse means! We trust in Jesus because he will not let us down," said Erin.

"That's right," said Dad. "When you trust Jesus you are saying you believe Jesus loves and cares for you. Also, trusting in Jesus makes you want to do good things for Him."

"Maybe God wants me to swim in a big pool of trust," smiled Erin.

"I think so," said Dad.

Your Turn

How do you show Jesus you trust him?

_____

_____

Prayer

Dear Jesus, help me show my trust in you. Help me to show I love and trust you by doing good. Amen.

Swim to Jesus

Help the girl swim to Jesus to show her trust in him.

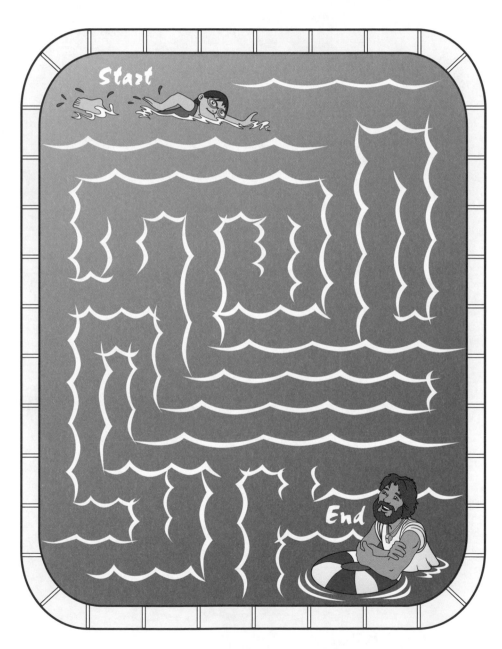

The answer is on page 239.

The Savior and Me

Jesus Saved Me

I love Jesus for the cross.

To us who are being saved [the cross] is the power of God.

~ 1 Corinthians 1:18

The Red Cross

Joy and her little sister, Grace, spent the day at a swimming pool. Grace made a mistake and swam into deep water. She began to sink!

"I'm drowning!" she called out in fear. "Help me, Joy."

Her big sister, Joy, was a very good swimmer. Swimming lessons called "Red Cross Safety" taught her to save drowning people. Joy swam right to her little sister, put out her arm and pulled her to safety.

Grace never let Joy forget that day. "I love you for the cross," she would say.

"The cross?" asked Joy. "You mean the Red Cross?"

"Yes!" said Grace.

Joy smiled at Grace. "You can love me for my Red Cross lessons, but that reminds me of the cross of Jesus. We all should love Him for the cross. We should love Jesus because He died on a cross for you and me. He paid for our wrongdoing with His life."

Grace looked into her big sister's eyes. "I love you for your Red Cross. But, most of all, I love Jesus for the cross."

Did you know that Jesus died because of the wrong that people do to themselves and others? He died for our sins. Sin is doing things that are wrong.

But here's the good news: when you are truly sorry for your sin, Jesus forgives you. When you are truly sorry you stop doing things your way and begin doing things God's way.

That's how Jesus pulls us to safety. Jesus saved our lives by dying. Now we can be with Him forever in heaven.

Your Turn

What does Jesus and the cross mean to you?

_____

_____

Prayer

Dear Jesus, I love you for the cross. I thank you for dying for me on the cross. Thank you, Jesus, for saving my life.

A Big Red Cross

Write your name and your friends' names on the cross. Pray for them each day. Ask Jesus to save them with his cross.

Love Shared

Jesus wants me to share his love with others.

Go into all the world and preach the gospel.

~ Mark 16:15

The Clouds

Two friends, Sierra and Laura, flew a kite on a windy day in March.

"Look at the cloud in the sky!" said Laura.

"Yeah, it looks like a sailboat," said Sierra.

Laura pointed to a cloud in a different direction. "Look at the one over there. It looks like a teddy bear," she said.

Laura said the clouds reminded her of something her Sunday school teacher had said: "Jesus left earth in a cloud."

"Jesus led his friends to a place called Bethany," Laura explained. "He lifted up his hands to the sky. As Jesus prayed for his friends, the clouds hid him."

"Wow," exclaimed Sierra. "What else happened?"

"Jesus said, 'The Holy Spirit will come and help you tell people about me,'" Laura continued. "Then suddenly, Jesus went up in the air as his friends watched. Two men in white appeared next to the friends. They were angels. They told the friends that Jesus would come back the same way he left.

"My Sunday school teacher said that Jesus wants us to share his love with others," Laura explained. "Jesus saved me so I should share his love everywhere."

Sierra liked hearing about Jesus and Sunday school. "Hey, Laura, can I come with you next Sunday?" she asked.

"That would be great!" smiled Laura.

Jesus sent the Holy Spirit to help his people tell others about him. He left so we would share his love with others. Tell as many people as you know about Jesus and his love!

Your Turn

1. Why did Jesus send the Holy Spirit when He went to heaven?

_____

_____

2. How can you tell others about Jesus?

_____

_____

Prayer

Thank you, Jesus, for sending the Holy Spirit to help us tell others about you. Holy Spirit, help me to share Jesus with others. Amen.

Heart Clouds

Think of friends and acquaintances you know who don't know Jesus. Write their names on the heart cloud below. Pray and ask God to help you bring them closer to him.

A Load for Jesus

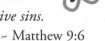

Jesus wants to forgive my sin.

[Jesus] has authority on earth to forgive sins.

~ Matthew 9:6

Sin Lifting

"Isn't he strong?" remarked Jenna as she watched the ballet dancer on TV lift the pretty ballerina over his head.

"He sure makes it look easy," said Dad. "But I know something the dancer can't lift."

"What's that, Dad?" asked Jenna.

"Sin," said Dad. "You see, Jesus is the only one who can lift sin. The Bible tells us about it. One day, some friends brought a sick man to Jesus. The friends wanted Jesus to help him get well. But the man wanted his sins forgiven first. His sins were like a heavy load on him. His sins made his heart feel very heavy and sad. Jesus loved the man and wanted to help him. When Jesus saw that the man was sorry for his sin, he said, 'Your sins are forgiven. Pick up your bed and walk.' The sick man did just what Jesus said!"

Doing wrong makes your heart feel heavy. It's like carrying a heavy backpack on your heart! But Jesus forgives sins and lifts them from your heart. He paid for all sins when he died on the cross. When you ask for forgiveness from Jesus, he takes that load away. Then you can start doing what God wants. That makes you happy inside.

Your Turn

1. Why do you think the man wanted Jesus to forgive him first?

_____

_____

2. What is sin?

_____

_____

3. What can you do you when you have sinned?

_____

_____

Prayer

Dear Jesus, forgive me for doing what I want to do rather than what you want me to do. Lift my sin up high and away from me. Come into my life and be my Lord and Savior. Amen.

The Jesus Lift

Let Jesus lift your sin! On the ballerina skirt below, write a sin that you need to let Jesus lift from you.

Thank You, Jesus

I am thankful that Jesus saved me.

[Jesus] loved me and gave himself for me.

~ Galatians 2:20

My Dream

Lizzy wrote a poem for the poetry contest at school:

> At times dreams make me laugh.
> At times dreams make me cry.
> It's fun to think about my dreams.
> As well as ask God why.

She had a special interest in dreams because she dreamt so often. Her dreams were colorful and bright.

Most of the time Lizzy had good dreams. However, one time she ended up in her parents' bed.

Mom said, "Lizzy, you had a nightmare."

"But it was so real," Lizzy said, frightened.

"That's how it is with dreams," said Dad, sitting up in bed. "It is like they are really happening. Now tell me about your dream, honey."

Lizzy laid down between her parents. "Well, I was inside my playhouse in the backyard when it caught on fire. I was trapped alone inside the house. Some boy saw that the house was on fire so he ran inside the burning house to get me out. I was fine, but I never saw the boy again. From then on I went around telling everyone, 'The boy saved me.'"

Mom smiled. "Lizzy that's exactly what Jesus did for you and me. Jesus loved us so much that he let people hurt him and nail him to a cross. He gave up his life on earth to save us from our sins. Just like in your dream, we will never forget the one who saved us. We will always be grateful to Jesus for what he did for us."

"Then I guess that dream wasn't so much of a nightmare after all!" Lizzy said.

Your Turn

How can you show Jesus you are thankful to him for dying for you?

_____

_____

Prayer

Dear Jesus, I don't want to forget all you have done for me. Help me to show you how thankful I am that you gave your life for me. Amen.

Creative Thanking

Design a creative "Thank You" page to thank Jesus for dying on the cross. Decorate the page for Jesus.

Spots of Sin

Jesus sees my sin.

"Look, the Lamb of God, who takes away the sin of the world!"

~ John 1:29

Sin Pox

"Ashley, it looks like these red spots are chicken pox!" said Mom. "Lets get you into bed now."

"Are chicken pox bad?" asked Ashley.

"You won't get sicker than you are now," said Mom. "You'll be back at school in a week."

Ashley scratched her stomach. "Can't we wash off these spots? They are so red and ugly."

Mom smiled, "Only time will erase those spots. You know, spots remind me of sin. When people are angry and unkind to others it's like they have sin pox. We may try to hide our sin, but the spots are there. And Jesus sees our spots even when we try to hide them."

Mom rubbed lotion on Ashley's spots as she continued to talk.

"Jesus loves us and wants us to tell him our sin. When we say, 'Jesus I have done wrong,' He says, 'I forgive you.' Then the sin spots go away!"

"I wish these chicken pox would go away like that!" said Ashley.

Your Turn

1. How does Jesus feel when he sees your sin spots?

_____

_____

2. Is it difficult for others to see your sin spots?

_____

_____

3. How does Jesus take away your sin spots?

_____

_____

Prayer

Jesus, thank you for helping me see my own spots. Forgive me for my sins and take away my sin spots. Amen.

A Girl's Sin Spots

Do you have sin spots? God takes away our sin spots if we ask him to forgive us. Erase the spots on the girl below by covering them with white tape or paint, or by drawing an X over each spot.

Jesus Cleanses Me

Jesus can make me clean.

"If you are willing, you can make me clean."

~ Mark 1:40

Running to Jesus

The Bible tells about a man who ran to see Jesus. He had spots on his body because of a sickness called "leprosy." No doctor could heal this bad illness.

Lepers were made to live outside the city with other lepers. So this man was left to beg for money outside the city walls. He was waiting to die.

Then the man heard that Jesus had been healing lepers. The man believed Jesus could help him. He hoped Jesus would come to his town.

One day, the man with spots heard Jesus was coming to his town! The man left his cave and walked to the city gate to wait for Jesus to pass by. When he finally saw Jesus, many people were gathered around him.

But the man with spots didn't care how many people were with Jesus. He ran up to him and fell at his dusty feet. The man said, "Lord, if you want to, you can make me clean."

Jesus reached out and touched the man and said, "I will make you clean."

All at once, one sore spot disappeared. Then another one disappeared, and another. Suddenly all his spots were gone! How happy the man was!

You may not have leprosy. But you probably have times when you show selfishness, envy, anger and hatred. That is like being sick with sin.

Just like the leper, we should run to Jesus when we have wrong attitudes or do wrong acts. The man's spots caused him to need Jesus. We need Jesus, too!

Your Turn

1. What are some spots in your life that cause you to run to Jesus?

_____

_____

2. What can Jesus do for your spots?

_____

_____

Prayer

Dear Jesus, everyone sins, but I know you can make me clean. Please forgive me for _____. Take my sin away. Amen.

A Jesus Run

The man in the story ran to meet Jesus when he saw him. You should run to Jesus when you do wrong, too. Help the leper at the gate find his way to Jesus.

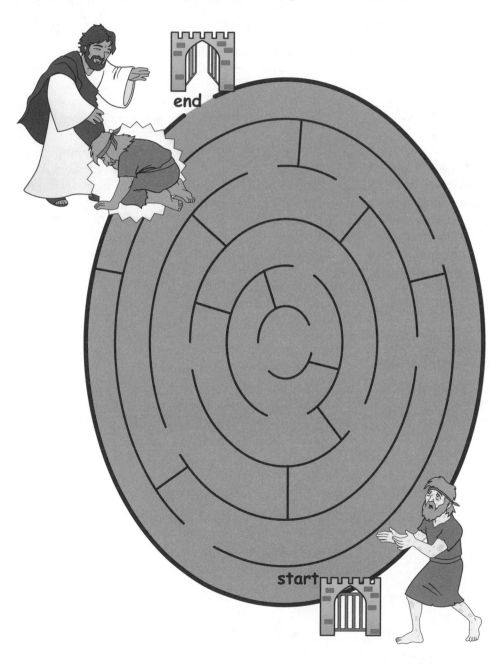

The answer is on page 239.

No Greater Love

Jesus died to save me.

Jesus came into the world to save sinners.

~ 1 Timothy 1:15

Mother's Love

Mother geese find hidden places to make their nests and lay their eggs. A mother goose takes special care of her eggs before they are hatched. A mother goose will leave the nest for very short times to search for food and water. If there's a storm, she will make sure the nest is completely covered with her feathers. After the baby geese hatch, the mother continues to protect them until they are old enough to be on their own.

Once a mother goose sat on her nest in tall, dry weeds. She kept four goslings hidden safely under her wings. But someone accidentally set fire to the field where the nest was built. The weeds around the nest began to burn, but the goose did not move. She wouldn't leave her babies. The mother sat on the nest as the fire burned the entire field of weeds. Her feathers burned and she died. But, the baby geese stayed alive and safe under her wings.

The mother goose saved those she loved, but she didn't save herself. The Bible says that Jesus died to save us. Jesus could have saved himself from death on the cross. Instead, he saved those he loved and didn't save himself. Jesus loves us like a mother animal loves her babies. There is no love greater than that!

Your Turn

1. Why did the goose die for her goslings?

_____

_____

2. Jesus gave his life for you. What should you give him?

_____

_____

Prayer

Thank you, Jesus, for dying on the cross for me. Thank you for saving me. Amen.

Wing Drawings

Draw yourself under the mother's wing to remind you Jesus saves.

A Willing Heart

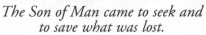

Jesus willingly died for me.

*The Son of Man came to seek and
to save what was lost.*

~ Luke 19:10

Heart of Love

The Fletcher family was on a summer vacation in the mountains. One day, they decided to take a drive to a nearby park. But as they were driving, their car slid off the road. Mom, Dad and their two kids were hurt.

Kind people passing by called for help. The ambulance arrived to take them to the hospital. But the ambulance could only hold three people, and there were four people in the Fletcher family.

"Leave me here and take my family first," said Dad. Happily, another ambulance soon arrived to bring Dad to the hospital, too.

It is easy to see this father's love for his family. He was willing to give his life for theirs.

Jesus had this same kind of love for us when he died on the cross. His heart of love made him willing to give his life. He didn't have to die on the cross. He could have saved himself. Instead, he chose to die in our place. Jesus' death saved us from our sins.

Your Turn

1. Why did the father choose to wait?

_____

_____

2. Why did Jesus choose to die for you?

_____

_____

Prayer

Thank you for dying for me. I want to show my love back to you by obeying and helping you. Amen.

Connect the Hearts Game

Connect the hearts for each letter to see what message they tell.

The answer is on page 239.

The Savior and Me

Jesus, I'm glad to be your child.

Dear friends, now we are the children of God.

~ 1 John 3:2

A Child of God

Rosa had no parents. They had died when she was a baby. So she lived in a special home for children without parents.

Rosa loved the adults who cared for her in the home. She had everything she needed. But the one thing she wanted most was a real family. She felt empty inside her heart without a family.

One day a man and woman visited the home where Rosa lived. The couple liked Rosa. Each time they came, they mostly talked to her. They visited Rosa many times and grew to love her very much.

"Soon we will come back for you and take you as our own child," they said. The couple wanted to adopt Rosa! She felt joy for the first time in her life. There was hope in her heart!

When the special day finally came, Rosa left the home to begin a new life with her adoptive parents. She was so happy!

When you come to know Jesus as Lord and Savior you are like Rosa because you are brought into a new family. You are adopted into God's big family! Just as the couple adopted the girl, you become one of God's children.

God doesn't take you away from your parents. He just adds you to his big family. Hope comes into your heart and you begin to understand God's ways.

Your Turn

1. Why are people happy when they come to know Jesus?

_____

_____

2. Have you been adopted by God yet?

_____

_____

Prayer

Dear God, thank you for sending Jesus to die for me so someday I can come to my new home in heaven. Amen.

My Adoption Papers

On that special day when you ask Jesus to forgive your sins once and for all, you are adopted into the family of God. Fill out the special adoption papers below. These papers say that you officially belong to God's family.

Savior & Me
Adoption Papers

For: _____

Date: _____

Church: _____

How did you find out about Jesus?: _____
_____

Grabbing Big Prayer

My Father in Heaven

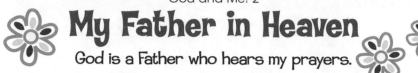

God is a Father who hears my prayers.

*"This, then, is how you should pray:
'Our Father in heaven.'"*

~ Matthew 6:9

A Faultless Father

Corrie ten Boom was a Christian who loved her dad very much. Her father owned a watch shop, and Corrie became the first woman watchmaker in Holland.

One day a war broke out near Corrie's town. Bad people called "Nazis" came to take over the town. The Nazis hated Jews and wanted to hurt them, but the Bible says the Jews are God's people. Some Jews came to Corrie and her family for help. So Corrie's family began hiding the Jews behind a wall in a secret room at their house.

After awhile, the Nazis found the hidden Jews. They arrested Corrie and her family. All of them were sent to prison. Corrie never saw her dad again.

Corrie was sent to a terrible work camp for women. But God helped her sneak in a Bible with her. Corrie held secret Bible studies in the camp.

God took care of Corrie in amazing ways. She turned to God in her time of trouble and knew He would hear her. Even though Corrie's earthly father was not with her, her heavenly Father cared for her every need. God heard Corrie's prayers and helped her leave the work camp.

God is different from your earthly father because he is faultless. He has the power to love you perfectly and hear your prayers. Your earthly father might love you very much, but it's your heavenly Father to whom you should pray.

Your Turn

1. What kinds of things do you worry about?

_____

_____

2. Do you think God can handle them? Why or why not?

_____

_____

Prayer

Father in heaven, thank you for listening to me when I pray. Thank you for caring for me and answering my prayers. I love you! Amen.

Faultless Father Features

Make a list that describes a faultless father. Everyone has faults and no one is perfect except our heavenly Father. Which of the things on your list tell about God? Let God be your faultless Father.

Faultless Father

1. love
2.
3.
4.
5.
6.

Blessed Be Your Name

I will praise God's name.

"...hallowed be your name."

~ Matthew 6:9

David's Songs

Robin heard her parents talking about their new city mayor.

"Oh, Carl Gruber grew up on my street when I was a girl," said Robin's mom. "I've known him for years."

Robin listened carefully to the praises her dad gave the new mayor. "He's very bright and he has many good ideas. He can do a lot of things well."

Then her mom added, "I know he will be helpful to this city as mayor. He is a wonderful man"

Robin was listening to someone's name being praised by her parents. The Bible tells of a boy named David who sang songs that praised God's name. He told others in song and prayer how great and holy God is. Sometimes David's songs were prayers asking God for help.

In Psalm 100, David prays to God, telling Him how great He is: "Worship the Lord with gladness; come before him with joyful songs." You can read more of David's prayers in the Bible book called "Psalms."

You can worship God when you pray. It's a prayer that says good things about God and His name.

Matthew 6:9 says "...hallowed be your name." That means that God's name is blessed. His name is good, right and pure, just as He is.

Your Turn

1. How do you think God feels when you offer praise prayers to him?

_____

_____

2. How do you feel when you pray praise and worship prayers to him?

_____

_____

Prayer

Dear Father in heaven, I praise you and worship you because you are good. Your name is holy. Help me to remember to keep your name special. Amen.

Praise God's Name Match-up

God's names tell us how special he is and how we should honor him. Look up the Scriptures below and draw a line to match the Scripture with the name for God described in that scripture. Pray these names back to God by saying, "God, you are the Shepherd of Israel," "You are the Prince of Peace," and so on.

Psalm 24:7   Shepherd of Israel

Psalm 80:1   Prince of Peace

Isaiah 9:6   King of Glory

Job   Holy God

37:23
                                               Creator

2 Corinthians 1:3

                                               God of all Comfort

Joshua 24:19

                                               The Almighty

Isaiah 40:28

The answer is on page 239.

Your Kingdom Come

I can be in God's kingdom

"...Your kingdom come."

~ Matthew 6:10

A Kingdom Girl

Casey's family goes to church every Sunday. She won a prize in Sunday school for having perfect attendance. Casey attends Wednesday night Bible club at church, and she never forgets to take her Bible. Casey even has taken unsaved friends to church with her. God must be so pleased with all that she is doing! Surely God will let her into the kingdom?

Melissa is a good girl. She has helped many people. At Thanksgiving, she served food with her family at the local homeless shelter. Melissa is also a reading buddy to a younger girl at school. That means she helps her learn to read. Not many girls her age do as much as Melissa does to help others. Surely God will let her into His kingdom?

Even though Casey and Melissa are doing many good things that God likes, they could still miss getting into God's kingdom. That's because only doing good things is not enough. God wants us to turn our lives over to him. Only when we let him guide us will he know that we want to live in his kingdom.

When Jesus taught us how to pray, He said, "Your kingdom come." He was talking about God's kingdom. God invites everyone to be a part of his kingdom.

Are you a Kingdom Girl? Do you know you will live with God in heaven forever? If not, stop now and pray, "Yes! I want to be in Your kingdom. I believe that Jesus died on the cross for me. I turn over my life to You."

Your Turn

1. Is everyone in the world a child of God and in his kingdom?

_____

_____

2. How do you think you can get into God's kingdom?

_____

_____

Prayer

Dear God, thank you for allowing me to take part in your kingdom. The part I like best about being in your kingdom is _____. Amen.

Kingdom Castle

God wants you to be in his kingdom. But how can you get into God's kingdom? Look inside the castle door and see how to get into God's kingdom. Will you go in? Draw your face in the window of the castle tower. Then draw the faces of others you know who aren't yet in God's kingdom.

Your Will Be Done

God's plans for us are perfect.

"...Your will be done on earth as it is in heaven."

~ Matthew 6:10

When My Plans Fail

Lora's dad had an out-of-town business meeting to attend. But instead of staying behind as they usually did, Lora, her sister, and her mom were going with Dad on his trip. Lora was excited!

The plan was that Dad would go to his meeting in the morning and then take the family to the zoo in the afternoon. Then they would relax by the hotel pool in the evening.

However, during the long car ride for the trip, Lora's sister came down with an earache. So instead of fun at the zoo and the pool, the family spent the whole day in a hospital waiting to see a doctor. Their plans for a fun afternoon and evening were ruined!

But Lora's family did spend time together. They prayed and trusted God to help them. The trip did not go the way they had planned, but it went God's way.

You probably make new plans every day. You arrange time with friends, classes and many other activities. But sometimes your plans don't work out. The only thing you can trust is that God's plans never fail. That's why it is important that his will be done, not yours. Doing things God's way means to trust that he has something even better for you when your plans fail. God's plans are perfect.

Your Turn

1. Why should you pray for God's plans to happen?

_____

_____

2. How do you think life on earth is different from life in heaven?

_____

_____

Prayer

Dear God, help me to want the things that you want. Let your plans happen on earth as they do in heaven. Show me how to trust your plans when mine go wrong. Amen.

My Six Prayers

Practice letting God's plans guide your prayers. Trace each of the five prayer areas below. As you trace, talk to God about each one.

PRAY   for help to do good things for others.

PRAY   for boldness to tell friends about Jesus.

PRAY   for help in being kind –
         even to those who are mean.

PRAY   for help in remembering to read the Bible.

PRAY   for help in obeying my parents.

PRAY   that when my plans don't work out,
         I will trust God's plans.

Give Us Today Our Daily Bread

I can ask God to supply my needs.

"Give us today our daily bread."

~ Matthew 6:11

Daily Bread

The next part of the Lord's Prayer says, "Give us today our daily bread." When Jesus said "give us our daily bread" He meant, "God, supply me with everything that helps me in my life such as: food, drink, clothing, shelter, health, friends and other things like these."

During Bible times, God's people in Israel learned that he gives us our daily bread. As they fled slavery in Egypt, they grabbed some baked bread for their journey. But with a long trip ahead they knew the bread wouldn't last.

The desert was hot, and soon the Israelites became tired and hungry. What would you do if you thought you might die of hunger? Well, the people fussed at God. They even told Moses they wanted to go back to the bad king in Egypt! They thought about all the food there and wished they could return.

God heard their fussing. He wasn't happy with them, but he loved them. He knew they needed their daily bread. So God told Moses to tell the people to go to sleep. When they woke up they would see that God had supplied for them.

Sure enough, the next morning the ground was covered with their daily bread. It was called "manna." The people were happy that God had taken care of them.

God takes care of you, too! He gives you your daily bread–even when you have a bad attitude. God wants to give you what you need.

Your Turn

1. Why do you think God wants to provide for you?

_____

_____

2. How do you think God feels when you complain about what He gives you?

_____

_____

Prayer

Dear God, I have things that I need. Thanks for loving me enough to want to provide for my needs. Right now I ask you to provide _____. Amen.

My Daily Bread

Bread is one of the most basic foods that we need. When Jesus taught us to pray, "Give us today our daily bread," He was saying, "ask me for the things that you need." God doesn't promise to give us everything we want, but he does give us what we need. Put an X over the pictures of the things you want instead of need. Look at the things you need and ask God for them.

Forgive Us Our Sins

I can ask God to forgive me.

"Forgive us our debts."

~ Matthew 6:12

The Sliver

Haley's father tore down an old cedar deck behind their house.

"Stay away from those boards," Haley's mom told her. "You could get wood slivers in your hands and feet."

Haley didn't obey her mothers warning. "Look, Mom! I have a sliver to show you," said Haley as she stuck out her finger.

Sure enough, Haley had a big wood sliver just under the skin in her pointer finger. Haley's mom could tell that Haley felt bad about not following directions. Mom assured Haley that it would be okay as she removed the sliver. Then Mom applied the healing cream.

But what if Haley had been too ashamed of not obeying? What if she had let the sliver stay there instead of bringing it to her mom right away? It could have gone deeper into her skin and become infected. And it would have been harder to remove. Haley showed that she believed her mom would help her.

Haley's hurt finger is like our lives. The longer we wait to pray for forgiveness of our sins, the worse we feel. Just like Haley's mom removed the wood, God takes away our sins and makes us feel better. God is always willing to forgive and heal us.

Your Turn

1. What should you do when you do something wrong?

_____

_____

2. How does sin change your friendship with God?

_____

_____

3. How can you know God has forgiven you?

_____

_____

Prayer

Dear God, I know I have done what I wanted to do, when I wanted to. I want to be forgiven. Thank you for forgiving me and taking away my pain. Amen.

Sliver-Free Fingers

Under the wood with slivers, write sins that you need to tell God. Draw a cross on the bandaged finger on the right. God forgives and heals you when you ask him!

My Slivers

_____

_____

_____

_____

As We Forgive Others

God will help me forgive others.

"As we also have forgiven our debtors."

~ Matthew 6:12

The Rich Ruler

As Gabrielle and her father were driving across town in their brand-new car, a woman's car ran into the back of them. When her dad took the car to the mechanic, he said it would cost $1,000 to fix it.

"You have to pay for my car to be fixed," Dad told the woman over the phone. But, when Dad found out she was a single mother with young children, he felt sorry for her. The woman didn't have enough money to fix her own car or his car.

So Gabrielle's dad decided to forgive the woman and what she owed him. He could have been very angry toward the woman. But instead, he knew God wanted him to forgive what was owed.

Jesus told a story to show how important it is to forgive others. You can read it in Matthew 18:21-35. Here's the same story with a modern twist:

A rich ruler was looking at his checkbook one day. He noticed a girl name Beth had borrowed money and not paid him.

"It's time to pay me back," he told Beth.

Beth shook her head sadly. She had used up all the money and couldn't pay it back.

"If you can't pay I'll sell your family and all you have," he told her.

Beth fell to her knees and begged the rich ruler for mercy. "I'll work hard for you and pay you back," said Beth.

The man thought for a moment. "You won't need to pay me after all. I'll forgive what you owe." Beth jumped for joy and was very happy.

Jesus told this story to show the importance of forgiveness. Jesus died on the cross to show that He forgives us. He wants us to forgive others, too.

Your Turn

1. What did it mean when Jesus died on the cross?

_____

_____

2. Look up Ephesians 4:32. What does God's Word say about forgiveness?

_____

_____

Prayer

Dear God, you forgive me all the time. Thank you for being ready to forgive me. Help me to be ready to forgive others just as you have forgiven me. Amen.

Forgiveness Steps

Try to figure out each step to forgiveness by filling in the blank letters on each step. Can you practice the steps when someone hurts you? Draw yourself on the steps.

The answers are on page 239.

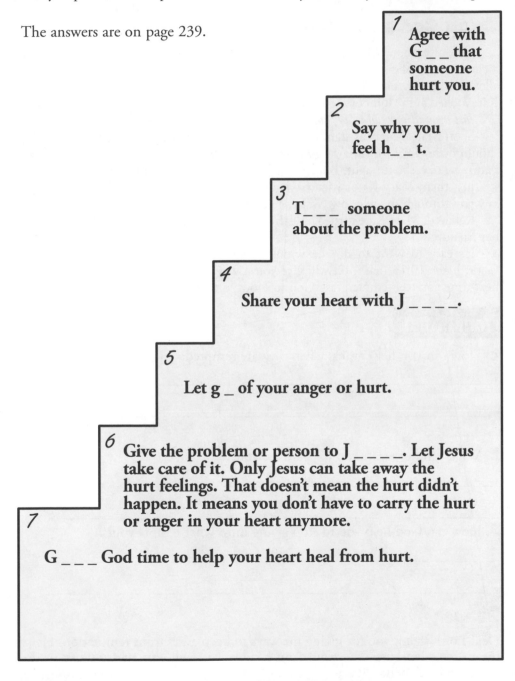

1 Agree with G _ _ that someone hurt you.

2 Say why you feel h_ _ t.

3 T_ _ _ someone about the problem.

4 Share your heart with J _ _ _ _.

5 Let g _ of your anger or hurt.

6 Give the problem or person to J _ _ _ _. Let Jesus take care of it. Only Jesus can take away the hurt feelings. That doesn't mean the hurt didn't happen. It means you don't have to carry the hurt or anger in your heart anymore.

7 G _ _ _ God time to help your heart heal from hurt.

Away From Temptation

God leads me away when I'm tempted to do wrong.

"And lead us not into temptation."

~ Matthew 6:13

Going God's Way?

One afternoon, Mary Kate was walking near her house when she came upon a candy store. She turned and stood in front of the window. Mary Kate was not allowed to eat sweets because her doctor said they would make her sick. But as Mary Kate looked at the lollipops, chocolate bars and gumballs, she began to get tempted.

Just a small piece of candy couldn't hurt, she thought as she opened the door.

Soon Mary Kate was standing in the middle of the store considering what she should do. *If I eat the candy, I'll be going against the rules and I'll get in trouble plus maybe get sick,* she thought. But the smell of that delicious candy was so wonderful!

Just then, Mary Kate's friend Wendy walked in the store. "Hey, Mary Kate. I saw you through the window. Want to go the park?"

Relieved, Mary Kate turned away from the candy and headed out the door with her friend.

It's easy to want to do the wrong thing at times. But the Bible says in 1 Corinthians 10:13 that God will give you a way out when you are tempted. The next time you feel tempted, ask God to show you the way out.

Your Turn

1. How can you help others when they are tempted?

_____

_____

2. What kind of temptation is hard for you?

_____

_____

3. How can God help you to stop giving in to what tempts you?

_____

_____

Prayer

Dear Lord, thank you for giving me ways to keep away from temptation. Help me to see what keeps me from you. I know you will give me strength to do what's right. Amen.

Big Temptations

With God's strength you can keep from being tempted by evil. Draw a line from the temptation on the left to how God helps you on the right.

When I am tempted to...

Make fun of someone who is different

Cheat when playing a game

Laugh at someone being teased

Use bad words when I'm angry

Watch TV shows that I'm not supposed to

Not clean up my room as told

Push toys under my bed

Stay outside and play too late

God helps me to...

be inside on time.

clean my room.

watch shows that honor God.

be kind to others, even if it's hard.

follow the rules.

use kind words.

put them away where they belong.

stand up for others.

Keep Us Free from Evil

God can lead me from evil.

"But deliver us from the evil one."

~ Matthew 6:13

Stay Away From Evil

Are you near or far from God? Activities you choose can lead you near to God or away from God and toward bad things.

Amber spent the night at her friend Monica's house. Monica's older sister and her friends wanted Amber and Monica to play a strange game. They turned off the lights, held hands and asked for dead people to talk to them. But Amber remembered Isaiah 8:19-20 in the Bible. It says not to talk to the dead. So Amber called her mom to take her home.

Ginger's aunt bought her a CD for her birthday. It had many songs about Jesus on it. Ginger began listening to it as she lay in bed at night. Soon, all her bad dreams stopped!

Holly watched a movie in which a girl hated her parents. In the movie, the girl talked back to her parents and fought with them. The next day, Holly was mad at her parents. She wanted to argue when they told her to pick up her room.

Being with Christians, praying and learning the Bible will help to keep you from evil. When Jesus died on the cross he fought Satan and won. We don't need to worry about Satan because Jesus has already won the battle over him. But we do need to stay near to God and run away from evil.

Your Turn

1. How can you tell if something will draw you to God or evil?

_____

_____

2. How can you help others stay away from evil?

_____

_____

Prayer

Dear God, thank you for sending Jesus to overpower evil. Thank you for your Word and the truth to fight evil. Keep me strong in the truth. Amen.

Near or Far From Evil

Look at the mountain of evil and the mountain of God. Draw a picture of yourself on top of the mountain where you want to be.

Putting It Together

Jesus teaches me to pray.

This, then, is how you should pray: "Our Father in heaven, hallowed be your name, your kingdom come, your will be done, on earth as it is in heaven. Give us today our daily bread. Forgive us our debts, as we also have forgiven our debtors. And lead us not into temptation, but deliver us from the evil one."

~ Matthew 6:9-13

Okay, Let's Pray!

When the disciples asked Jesus to teach them to pray, He gave them "The Lord's Prayer" (see above). But Jesus doesn't want us to always pray those same words. He gave them so we would understand what should be in a prayer.

Could you picture having a best friend without talking to her? Prayer is as real as any phone call, letter or e-mail. Prayer makes your friendship strong with God.

Not sure if you have a reason to pray? James 5:13-16 tells some times to pray such as when you are in trouble, when you are happy and when you are sick. You can also pray to show your faith, to pray for others and to tell God your sins. When you're worried, upset or frightened and even when something good happens, you can pray. Yes, you can pray any time about anything. God loves to spend time with you!

Okay, then, let's pray!

Your Turn

1. Why did Jesus like to pray?

_____

_____

2. Why did Jesus create the Lord's Prayer?

_____

_____

3. Where, why and when should you pray?

_____

_____

Prayer

Pray the Lord's Prayer. Say "Amen" at the end.

The Lord's Prayer Puzzle

Color the Lord's Prayer puzzle below. For fun, use the color key to create a beautiful picture. God's big prayer is beautiful to him. It is a reminder that we can always talk to him.

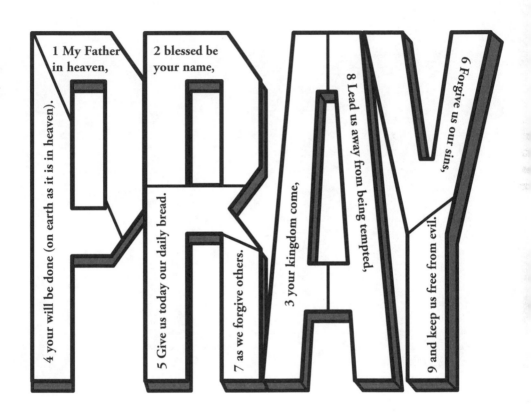

1 My Father in heaven,

2 blessed be your name,

4 your will be done (on earth as it is in heaven).

5 Give us today our daily bread.

7 as we forgive others.

3 your kingdom come,

8 Lead us away from being tempted,

6 Forgive us our sins,

9 and keep us free from evil.

1 Red **2 Yellow** **3 Blue**

4 Green **5 Orange** **6 Purple**

7 Pink **8 Your choice!** **9 Brown**

Prayer Is...

Every Breath a Prayer

Prayer is...like breathing.

Let everything that has breath praise the LORD.

~ Psalm 150:6

Prayer Breath

Tiffany's dad blew up 10 balloons for her birthday party.

"The more you blow, the bigger the balloon gets," Tiffany told her dad. But the larger the balloon grew, the more out of breath her dad became!

Mary went to the doctor because she had the flu. The doctor told her to take three deep breaths. Then he listened to her lungs.

"Her breathing is good," he told her parents.

Ashley's gym class ran laps on the track behind the school. After the first lap, Ashley said, "I'm out of breath."

Taking air into your lungs and letting it out again is called "breathing." Breathing is something you do without thinking—and that's the way prayer should be.

Just like when you blow up a balloon, the more often you pray, the bigger you get for God. The Bible even says, "Let everything that has breath praise the Lord."

Praying was like breathing to Jesus. He prayed for the sick and hurting. Jesus saw prayer needs everywhere he walked. His prayers were like breathing life into the dying hearts of people.

Let prayer become like breathing for you. Make every breath be a prayer for someone.

Your Turn

1. How was praying like breathing for Jesus?

_____

_____

2. What do you see around you that can become a prayer?

_____

_____

Prayer

Dear God, teach me to pray as I breathe. Let me pray without thinking about it. Show me people who need prayer. Show me places that need prayer. Amen.

The Breathing Prayer

Write the names of people or places you can pray for in the girl's breath (turn your book first so the girl is right-side up).

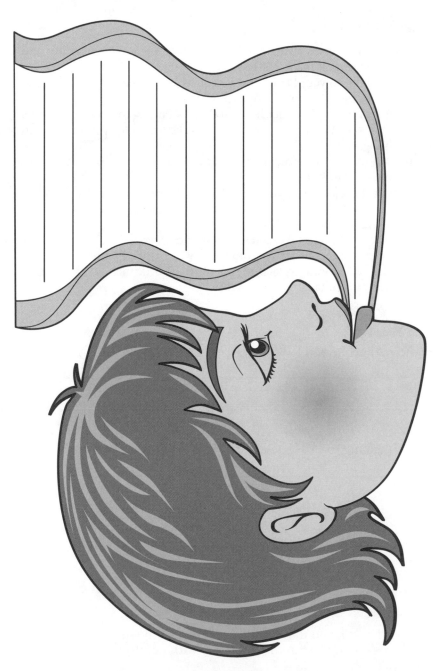

Love Talking

Prayer is...talking to someone you love.

As the Father has loved me, so have I loved you.

~ John 15:9

A Bedtime Talk

Bedtime was Carrie's favorite part of the day. She loved snuggling and reading a book with her dad. It made her feel loved.

"I love talking to you, Dad," said Carrie as he tucked her in each night.

"I love you, too," he would say back to her.

Carrie's dad liked telling her how God loves talking to her, too. "God loves you more than I love you," said Dad. "That means he wants for you to talk with him in prayer each night."

"How do you talk to someone you can't see?" Carrie asked. "We can't see God, but we know he is in heaven."

Dad pulled the covers up and over Carrie. "Let's have a bedtime talk with God right now," he said.

"I'll pray first," Carrie said.

Talking to God is like talking to someone you love. Just tell him what is on your mind and in your heart. After you pray, you will be filled with comfort and joy.

Carrie looked forward to talking to her dad at bedtime. God loves us and wants us to look forward to talking to him, too.

Your Turn

1. Is there someone you look forward to talking to?

_____

_____

2. How is talking to God like talking to someone you love?

_____

_____

3. How does talking to God give you strength?

_____

_____

Prayer

Dear God, I thank you that I can talk to you. Although I can't see you, I know you're there. Talking to you fills my heart with comfort and joy. Amen.

Heart Phone

Write on the receiver of the phone below the name of someone you love and with whom you can pray.

Joyful Praying

Prayer is...joy and fun.

In all my prayers for all of you,
I always pray with joy.

~ Philippians 1:4

Prayer Is Fun

Zoe was talking at school with her friend Lily.

"Church was really fun yesterday," she said.

"No way! You mean church is fun?" Lily asked, surprised.

Zoe had invited Lily to her church many times, but she hadn't come...yet.

"My Sunday school class is a blast. We have fun praying together," Zoe said.

"What's so fun about praying?" asked Lily.

"Sometimes we go prayer walking," Zoe explained. "You just put on your shoes and start walking. It's walking and praying for the people and things you see. Believe me, it's fun! We play all sorts of games that teach us how to pray."

Zoe felt such joy in just talking about her Sunday school class. But Lily wasn't sure how prayer could be fun.

"I don't pray that often. When I do pray, it isn't much fun," Lily said. "But it sounds fun when you talk about it."

Zoe smiled as she reached down to tie her shoe. "When you know Jesus, he teaches you to pray. Besides, praying is meant to be enjoyable."

"Can I go prayer walking with you sometime?" asked Lily.

"Sure!" said Zoe. "Let's prayer walk on our way home from school today. You'll see how talking to God can be fun. It is fun to talk to him no matter where or when."

Your Turn

1. Do you have a friend with whom you can have fun praying?

_____

_____

2. What are some fun ways you can pray?

_____

_____

Prayer

Thank you, God, that I can take joy in prayer. Teach me to enjoy the things you enjoy. Teach me to pray with joy. Let me look forward to prayer. Amen.

Prayer Squares

Look at the prayer squares below. Finish coloring each square and pray for what the square shows.

Sweet Prayers

Prayer is...something sweet.

God has surely listened and heard my prayer.

~ Psalm 66:19

The Berry Bushes

"Look, sweet berries!" said Kate as she and her sister, Nicole, hiked in the woods behind their house.

"Let's eat some," Nicole said.

Kate wasn't sure about eating wild berries. "Are you sure they are sweet?" she asked.

"No," Nicole said, "but, let's try one and see."

Nicole plopped one into her mouth. "Mmm, Kate, these are sweet!" she said.

Kate began piling berries into her shorts' pockets. "I'll bring some for Grandma," she said. "She's been sick and can't get out much."

"Good idea!" said Nicole. "It would be sad not to give away something so sweet."

When you pray, you are giving away something sweet to God. The Bible says that prayer is sweet to God. That is why he loves our prayers so much!

Prayer can be a sweet gift of prayer and worship, too. Use the words below as a sweet prayer to God:

> Dear God, Your beauty shines everywhere on earth.
> You love me so much!
> You sent Jesus to be my friend.
> You sent Your Spirit to keep me from missing You and Jesus.
> You are full of love and You love me when I do bad.
> You take my sins away and let me start again.
> How can I ever thank You and tell You I love You?

Your Turn

1. What do you love to eat that is sweet?

_____

_____

2. Name someone who needs your sweet prayers. Pray for that person!

_____

_____

Prayer

Dear God, I praise you and worship you. Show me how to send sweet prayer your way. Amen.

Berry Bush Puzzle

Find and circle the words "Sweet Prayers" hidden in the berry bush below.

P K S W E E T
S R H D E W X
P R A Y E R S
W U R T O E P
W O E R A T Y

The answer is on page 239.

Friendly Prayers

Prayer is...talking to my friend Jesus.

*I have called you friends, for everything that I learned
from my Father I have made known to you.*

~ John 15:15

Backyard Prayers

Megan was having a birthday sleepover with her friends Ashley, Paige, and Rachel. Megan's dad had set up the family tent in the backyard.

"Don't forget your sleeping bag," Megan reminded each girl.

Megan had planned events for the evening. After the card game, board game and a movie with popcorn, Megan planned to ask the girls to pray with her. The four friends were used to praying together on their elementary prayer team at church.

But that night, things didn't work out as Megan had hoped. One by one, the girls fell asleep. Disappointed, Megan ended up praying alone.

"That sounds like Jesus praying in the garden," Megan's mom said the next day as Megan told her what had happened. "You weren't alone–your friend Jesus was there with you!"

"What do you mean?" asked Megan.

"Jesus and his friends camped out at an olive garden called Gethsemane," said Mom. "'Stay here, while I go pray,' Jesus told the guys. Some stayed, but Peter, James and John went with him. After Jesus prayed, he got up and went back to Peter, James and John and found them sleeping. 'Couldn't you stay awake for one hour?' Jesus asked Peter. Then Jesus went back to pray alone."

"That does sound like my friends!" said Megan. "At least I know Jesus is there when I pray. I can always count on Him to be awake."

Your Turn

1. What does it mean to be a friend?

_____

_____

2. How do you think Jesus felt when he found his friends sleeping?

_____

_____

Prayer

Dear Jesus, I love you and pray that you will always be my friend. I know when I pray, you'll be there. Friends are nice, but you are my real friend. Amen.

Sleep Over Prayer Snacks

Write a short prayer in the girls' popcorn bowl in the center.

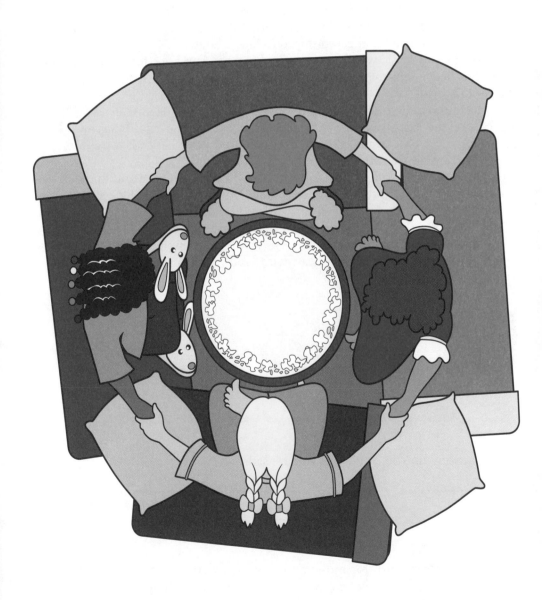

Prayer Music

Prayer is...singing.

I will sing to the LORD all my life.

~ Psalm 104:33

Songs of Prayer

Ann's heart was sad because her dad didn't know Jesus. In fact, he wouldn't go to church on Sundays with Ann and her mom. She knew her dad was a good man, but he was also stubborn and wanted to do things his way. Ann and her mom missed having him with them as they worshiped in God's house.

Listening to music was the one thing that gave Ann hope for her dad. Music lifted her heart! Ann told her mom, "Singing is like praying. It makes my heart happy and joyful."

Music also caused Ann to think of ways to pray for her dad. As she sang "Jesus Loves Me," she exchanged the word "me" with "Dad." So she sang, "Jesus loves Dad this I know…" That reminded her how much God loved her dad. It was a prayer to God saying she wanted Dad to belong to God's family.

Singing is like talking to God in song. Many songs are from words in the Bible. God loves hearing Scripture sung back to him. If you ever feel alone, just sing. You don't have to have a good voice to sing. King David said, "I will sing to the Lord all my life." He knew how to sing as a prayer to God.

God made music for us and he wants us to sing. Worshiping at your church and singing new songs will feed your heart with God's love. A song is prayer to God's ears.

Your Turn

1. Why do you think singing helps us feel God's love?

_____

_____

2. What song do you sing when you are sad?

_____

_____

Prayer

Thank you, dear Lord, for music and your wonderful love. You comfort me when I'm sad. You are the one who puts a song in my heart. I love to sing a prayer to you. Amen.

Heart Songs CD

Write the name of your favorite worship song on the CD below. Sing a prayer to God by singing the song.

Broken Heart Prayers

Prayer is...giving away hurts.

Cast your cares on the LORD and he will sustain you.

~ Psalm 55:22

Humpty Dumpty

Jessica felt like she had a big crack in her heart. "Why did my daddy have to leave?" she asked her grandma.

Grandma gave Jessica a big hug. "I know you feel very, very sad and crying is normal. Honey, you'll feel better in time as your heart heals. Right now your heart is broken because of your parents' divorce," said Grandma. "A broken heart can heal. But, until then, I'll be here to listen to you any time you need me. Remember the rhyme Humpty Dumpty?"

"Yes," said Jessica looking at Grandma with tears in her eyes.

Grandma and Jessica said the rhyme together: "Humpty Dumpty sat on a wall. Humpty Dumpty had a great fall. All the king's horses and all the king's men couldn't put Humpty together again."

Grandma smiled as she wrapped her arms around her granddaughter. "Jesus is the only one who can put Humpty Dumpty back together again," said Grandma. "Jesus is the only one who can put your broken heart together again, too."

Grandma brushed Jessica's hair back behind her ears. "The Bible says he will never leave you or forsake you. This problem isn't your fault, honey. Give your hurt away to God and in time you will heal."

"Can we pray now?" asked Jessica.

"Sure," said Grandma. "We'll pray together as much as you want. Let's pray God will heal all the hurts in our family."

Jesus knew to give his hurts to God, even when soldiers nailed him to the cross. Jesus prayed for the soldiers as they pushed nails into his hands and feet. He was hurting, but he gave his hurt to God. Jesus died so we could give him our hurts. He is listening to our prayer and ready to heal broken hearts and hurt lives.

Your Turn

Who can put our broken hearts together again?

_____

_____

Prayer

Dear Jesus, I give you my hurts today. Help me to remember you love me. Show me how to heal my hurts as I pray. Amen.

Humpty Dumpty's Wall

Look up the Bible story from Humpty Dumpty's wall. Read it with your parents. What caused the people in the story to feel hurt? What happened to take away their hurt? Color Humpty!

LUKE 15:11-32

Prayer and Good News

Prayer is...turning bad news into good news.

We are bringing you good news.

~ Acts 14:15

When News Is Bad

Tess was watching the evening news on TV. The stories were about robbers and storms. The news was all bad news.

"Mom, why is news always bad?" she asked.

"It isn't always bad," said Mom. "I know it seems that way sometimes, but even bad news can be turned to good when we pray. You see, God is in control of all that happens. The Bible says, 'It is God who rules over the affairs of man.' That means he can take what seems bad and make it good."

Tess thought for a moment. "I guess we should really pray when news is bad," she said.

"That's right," said Mom. "There are many stories in the Bible of bad news being turned into good news. Here's one.

"One day, Jesus and his friends went for a ride in a boat. Jesus' friends rowed while Jesus slept. At first, the wind gently blew and the waves splashed. Soon the wind blew stronger and the waves splashed bigger and bigger. Jesus' friends rowed harder and harder as Jesus slept on. They became afraid and began to yell for help. The storm was very bad news! But Jesus woke up with good news. He stood up in the boat. He looked at the wind and the waves and he said, 'Be still.' Jesus' friends looked at each other and asked, 'Who is this Jesus? Even the wind and the waves obey him.'"

Mom turned off the TV and called everyone for dinner. "Jesus took what looked like bad news and turned it into good news," she told Tess. "His friends cried out to him for help and he answered. When there is bad news, we should pray for good news. We can pray and ask for God to turn bad situations into good ones."

Your Turn

What should you do when you are in the middle of bad news?

_____

_____

Prayer

Thank you, Jesus, for answering prayer with good news. You are kind and full of mercy. You are in charge of the bad and good news. Amen.

Bad News Prayer Boat

Pray about some bad news as you finish coloring the boat below. Ask God to turn the bad into good.

Praying in Jesus' Name

Prayer is...praying in Jesus' name.

My father will give you whatever you ask in my name.

~ John 16:23

What's In a Name?

Dad led the family in prayer. At the end of the prayer, he said, "In Jesus' name I pray."

"Daddy, why do you say, 'In Jesus' name' when you pray?" asked Victoria.

"I'll tell you a story to explain it to you," said Dad.

"A girl named Beth loved her grandma very much. Each December, they made Christmas cookies together. Beth's grandmother also taught her to sew. But Beth's grandma became ill. The doctors said she would die soon.

"One day Grandma called Beth to her house. She asked Beth for paper and pencil. Then she slowly wrote out a note that said, 'I want you to have my favorite cuckoo clock when I die.' Grandma signed her name and Beth stuck the note in her coat pocket.

"After Grandma died, Beth asked her mom about the clock. She was surprised to find that the clock promised to her had already been given to her aunt.

"'But Grandma wanted me to have the clock,' she cried. Then she remembered the note in her coat pocket. Beth showed the note to her parents. Her parents saw Grandma's name at the end of the note. When they read the name, they showed it to the aunt. She quickly gave the clock to Beth."

"Wow," said Victoria.

"The note was written in Grandma's name," said Dad. "Her name on the letter told who was in charge of giving away the clock. That's why Beth received the clock. In the same way, we remind ourselves that Jesus is in charge when we pray in his name."

Your Turn

1. Why did Beth get the clock when she showed the paper?

_____

_____

2. Why should we pray in Jesus' name?

_____

_____

Prayer

Lord Jesus, thank you for letting me pray in your name. Your name is the best name! Amen.

Cuckoo Clock Prayers

On the stationery below, write a prayer and sign it "In Jesus name."

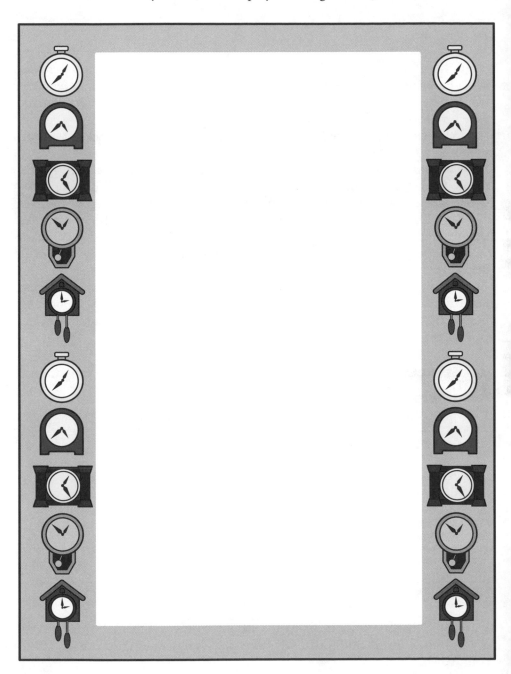

Calling on God

Prayer is...calling on the Lord.

The LORD will hear when I call to Him.

~ Psalm 4:3

God's Ears

Bess had many troubles. She had told a lie to her parents. Her friends were mad at her for being mean and they didn't want to be her friend anymore. She even broke her grandmother's favorite candy dish. To add to her troubles, Bess' school grades were very bad.

Kelly had troubles, too. Her sister was sick. Her dad's company closed. Friends were mean to her for no good reason.

Sometimes trouble comes because you are selfish or you do not try hard to follow God. Other times, trouble can happen when you haven't done anything wrong. Either way, God's ears are open and waiting for us to tell him our troubles.

King David said, "The Lord will hear when I call to him." King David had troubles, too. Some of his troubles were his own doing. But he knew that God's ears would hear him. He knew God could help change things. David knew God could help change his heart, too.

Fear and worry end when you feel God's love in prayer. Bess needed to change her actions. She needed to call on God to help her to change her behavior. Kelly needed to call on God to set her free from worry. God can help in any situation if you call on him through prayer. God's ears are always open!

Your Turn

1. Is it wise to call on God for help in times of trouble? Why or why not?

_____

_____

2. What can happen when you pray?

_____

_____

Prayer

Dear God, thank you for helping me with my troubles. I thank you for hearing my prayers. I am thankful that your ears are always waiting for me to talk to you. Amen.

Full Ears

Fill God's ears with your troubles. Write concerns inside God's ears below. Pray and ask God for help.

God's Ears

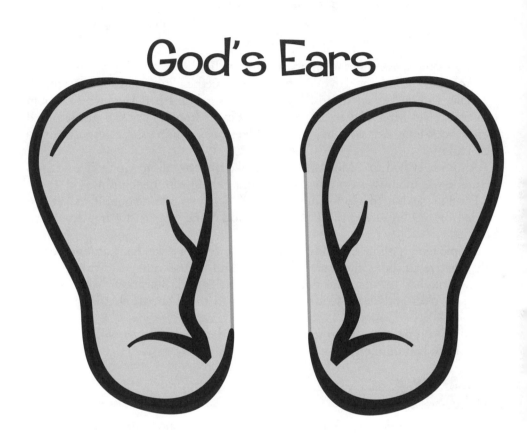

Praying and Thinking Right

Prayer is...flying free from bad thoughts.

If anything is excellent or praiseworthy –
think about such things.

~ Philippians 4:8

Flying Free

Haley's mom asked her to empty the dishwasher.

"You gotta be kidding! I'm in the middle of something important," Haley replied.

Haley's mom looked surprised. She had never heard her daughter answer in such a way. But Mom had an idea of where it came from! Haley had just returned from a week-long visit with her cousins. Her cousins didn't speak respectfully to their parents.

Also, Haley had told Mom she didn't make time to talk to God while she was away. She was too busy swimming, hiking and talking with her cousins.

Praying–talking to God–is important. When you allow yourself to get too worried or too busy, you don't pray. But God wants you to fly free from bad thinking.

People tend to think like those around them. So when you hang around people with negative attitudes, they rub off on you. And it's the same way with ungodly music, books and movies. Your thinking will be changed. But prayer will help your mind stay clear and clean. God will help you to think about what is important and good.

When you pray, you learn to think right and do right. Prayer will help you to fly free from bad thinking!

Your Turn

1. What can you do if someone begins to gossip to you about someone else?

_____

_____

2. How can you keep your thinking on the right track?

_____

_____

Prayer

Dear God, I pray you would help me to keep my mind clean. Lord, clean my mind as I pray and talk to you. I confess I have let myself think bad thoughts. I want my mind to be filled with your peace. Amen.

Flying Girl Maze

Follow the girl as she prays toward right thinking.

The answer is on page 240.

No More Fear

Prayer is...praying against fear.

I will fear no evil, for you are with me.

~ Psalm 23:4

Sleeping In Peace

Jordan was a busy girl during the day. Many activities kept her in constant motion. So, at night she was very tired and wanted to sleep.

However, Jordan was afraid at night. She wanted to leave on a light every night.

One night Jordan's dad noticed her light was on after he had tucked her into bed and turned out the light. He stuck his head in her bedroom door.

"Jordan," he asked, "why are you still awake?"

Jordan was tired of keeping her fear a secret. "Dad, I'm afraid!" she said.

"Afraid of what?" Dad asked.

"I don't know exactly," she answered. "I see shadows and feel afraid inside."

Dad sat at the foot of her bed. "Well, let's see here...is Jesus your Savior and friend?"

"Yes!" replied Jordan.

"Then he wants to help you with your fear. Because you're his, you can depend on him whenever you are afraid. Remember, when you sleep at night you're not alone."

Dad fluffed her pillow. "Also," he continued, "Jesus is there to protect you even in the dark. He is greater and more powerful than any bad thing. Talk to God when you're afraid. Tell him you're afraid and ask him to help you."

"What else can I do?" asked Jordan.

"You can pray Psalm 4:8. I'll pray it with you right now. 'Dear Jesus, I will lie down and sleep in peace, for you alone, O Lord, make me dwell in safety.'"

Jordan hugged her dad. "I feel better already," she said.

If you have trouble going to sleep at night, try thinking good thoughts and Scriptures you know. Never watch scary movies, especially before bed. And trust God and depend on Him for everything. He will protect you.

Your Turn

How do you keep from being afraid at night?

_____

_____

Prayer

Dear God, keep me from my fear. Train me in your ways so I will pray when I'm afraid. Amen.

My Scary List

Make a list of the things that scare you. Make another list of the things you can do to take away your fears. (Draw pictures or write the words.)

Things that scare me...

Take-away List

Praying and Drawing Closer to God

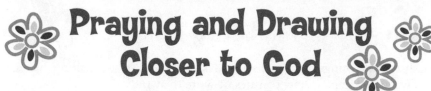

Prayer is...like a fan.

Fan into flame the gift of God, which is in you through the laying on of my hands.

~ 2 Timothy 1:6

Fanned Hearts

Betsy's family loved building a fire when they went camping. They built a blazing fire with just a few small sticks. Betsy's dad would throw a lit match onto the small pile of twigs. Then Betsy and her brother would blow on the fire with fans made from paper. Air from the fan caused the fire to grow bigger and bigger. Then Dad could add bigger pieces of wood. As Betsy and her brother fanned, Dad kept adding wood. The fire kept growing bigger and bigger until flames soared high.

That's what prayer is like! Praying is a fan on your heart helping you to be strong for Jesus. Prayer fans the flame of God that is in your heart when you first know him as Lord and Savior.

Prayer is also a fan that causes you to want to read your Bible. It causes you to want to go to church and be with your friends. Prayer makes your heart draw closer to God.

Prayer even causes you to want to help others. Prayer fans a desire to be hot rather than cold for Jesus. Prayer causes your talents and gifts to grow so you can serve God better.

Fan the flame of God in your heart through prayer. That is how you grow into a girl who serves God.

Your Turn

1. What can a fan over your heart do?

_____

_____

2. Do you want a hot or cold heart for God?

_____

_____

Prayer

Dear God, as I pray, let my heart be fanned. As I talk to you, fan into flame my talents and gifts that help me serve you better. Amen.

Fanned Flames

Fan the flames below by coloring the fire. Write short sentence prayers on the logs.

God, I pray my family will...

I pray You will help me...

Dear God teach me...

Dear God help me to...

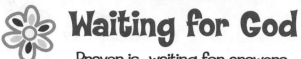 

Waiting for God

Prayer is...waiting for answers.

I waited patiently for the LORD; he turned to me and heard my cry.

~ Psalm 40:1

Wait, Wait, Wait

Do you get tired of waiting for Christmas or your birthday? Do you get tired of waiting for a friend to come out and play? Waiting for parents to answer your questions can take time, too!

Sometimes it's hard to wait when you really want something. We often want people to hurry up and give us what we ask. Sometimes we ask God to hurry up and give us what we ask, too. But God is never in a hurry. He always wants what's best. He knows when the time is right.

Jennifer's friend Kelly didn't know Jesus. Jennifer began praying that Kelly would come to know him. She prayed and she prayed. Jennifer prayed for one whole year! That seemed like forever to her! But one day God did answer her prayers. At Bible school, Kelly came to know Jesus as her Lord and Savior. Jennifer was so happy! She was glad she never gave up.

Kim prayed for God to give her a new friend when she moved to a new neighborhood. God answered her quickly. One week later, she met her new friend, Ruth. They became best friends.

Lauren prayed when her cat Patches was lost. She prayed for three weeks. Then one day she heard Patches meowing at the back door. She was so thankful!

Sometimes God holds off on his answers so he can take the praise for the answer. Other times he makes us wait so we will pray some more. God also says no at times. That is because He always knows what's best.

Your Turn

1. When have you had to wait for God to answer your prayers?

_____

_____

2. Name someone in the Bible who had to wait for God to answer a prayer.

_____

_____

Prayer

Dear God, I want to be able to wait for you to answer my prayers. I will trust you to hear and answer me when I call on you. Amen.

Clock Talk

Make the face of the clock below. Write in the numbers, and make the hands. Let the clock remind you that sometimes you must wait for God to answer your prayers.

Prayer Painting!

Prayer Painting

I can paint a prayer picture for God.

*Jesus told his disciples...that they
should always pray and not give up.*

~ Luke 18:1

Beautiful Prayers

Kim loved to paint! Almost every day she asked her parents if she could get out her paints.

Watercolors were Kim's favorites. Red, yellow, blue, and green were her favorite colors. Kim could spend hours with a paintbrush in her hand and never get tired. She used bright colors when she felt happy and dark colors when she felt sad.

Kim's parents even let her paint on the walls of their basement. After a week, the walls were covered with faces of family and friends. Her work was beautifully displayed for all to see.

Kim's mom put Kim's paintings in special frames. Everyone loved Kim's pictures because they came from her heart. They were created with great feeling and creativity.

Did you know that praying to God is like painting? Just as Kim's paintings were beautiful to her family, prayer is beautiful to God. Paintings please the one looking at them as our prayers please God.

Use your heart as a paintbrush to give your prayers to God. Prayer painting is brushing thoughts, ideas and problems onto the walls of heaven. Your prayers are beautiful to God and he wants to hear from you. So splash your prayers onto the walls of heaven.

Your Turn

1. Why are your prayers beautiful to God?

_____

_____

2. How is your heart like a paintbrush for prayer?

_____

_____

Prayer

Dear God, thank you for letting me paint my prayers on the walls of heaven. I like to paint my prayers on your walls. Thank you, God, for hearing my prayers and then answering them. Amen.

My Prayer Mural

Use markers or watercolors to paint a picture of a prayer you want to pray on the wall below.

Persistent Prayer

God answers my prayer.

He hears the prayers of the righteous.

~ Proverbs 15:29

Step Up

Hey, girls, step up and become a persistent prayer! To "persist" means to keep doing something again and again. So if you are a persistent prayer, that means you will keep praying again and again. Don't give up on prayer–step up!

In Luke 18:1, Jesus told his disciples they should pray and not give up. Sometimes when life gets hard, you might pray but soon give up. You might think your prayers aren't being heard. God hears each and every prayer. He wants to answer you when you call out to him. But God likes it when you persist in prayer.

Jesus told his disciples a story to teach them to persist in prayer. His story was about a widow who went to see a judge. Her enemies kept bothering her. She wanted the judge to do something about it. Over and over, the judge said no to her. But she didn't stop asking him for help. The widow went back to the judge many times.

Then one day the judge said, "Because this widow has been so persistent, I will see that she is treated fairly."

Jesus explained to his disciples that God hears those who pray to him. He will see that they get what they need.

God likes when you pray to him. He wants you to be a persistent prayer. So step up, girls, and persist in prayer!

Your Turn

1. What made the widow so persistent with the judge?

_____

_____

2. What keeps you going back to God in prayer?

_____

_____

Prayer

Dear God, I thank you that I can come to you over and over again in prayer. You never get tired of me! That is so nice of you! I will start stepping up and persisting in prayer. Amen.

Prayer Steps

Write prayers on the steps. Pray and ask God to answer your prayers.

1. _____

_____

_____

2. _____

_____

_____

3. _____

_____

_____

Prayers Set in Stone

My prayers are important to God.

The LORD has heard my cry for mercy; the LORD accepts my prayer.

~ Psalm 6:9

Stones of the Past

Dana's dad worked in the town stone mine. When school was out, she enjoyed going to work with him. Watching her dad scoop giant stones was great fun for her. Riding in the big truck was a treat!

After a morning of work, Dana, and Dad ate lunch together. As they ate, Dad told her about stones. First, he told her how stones last for many, many years.

"In Bible times, small stones were used as weapons. A boy, David, used five smooth stones to kill a giant, Goliath," Dad said.

He also told Dana how Bible people sharpened stones into knives. "Larger stones were used to cover wells and close the mouths of caves," he said.

Dana listened carefully as Dad told how stones were stacked in special places. They did this to remember how God had answered their prayers.

"Jesus described himself as a stone that the builders rejected," said Dad.

"Didn't God write in stone?" asked Dana.

"Yes!" said Dad. "God wrote the Ten Commandments in stone for Moses."

"Wow!" said Dana, "I would like to write in stone, too."

Dad took his hammer and pick from his backpack. "Let's write something in one of those stones now," he said.

As they worked, Dad said, "Our prayers to God are like stone. They stay with him forever. That's because our prayers are important to God."

"Let's write, 'I love You, God!'" said Dana. "And let's pray before we go back to work."

Your Turn

1. What did you learn in the story about stones?

_____

_____

2. Why do you think Jesus was called the living stone?

_____

_____

Prayer

Dear God, thank you for the living stone, Jesus. Thank you for answering my prayers. I know my prayers are important to you because you love me. Amen.

My Prayer Stone

Create your own prayer stone below. Write two things you want to tell God in prayer.

Armed Girls

I'm in God's prayer army.

Join with me in suffering, like a good soldier of Christ Jesus.

~ 2 Timothy 2:3

Walls Can Fall

"How is Daddy's army like God's army?" Audrey asked her grandma. Audrey's dad was a soldier in the military.

"Your daddy's army fights to keep our country safe," said Grandma. "They also fight so we can worship God the way we want. Guns are used to fight the enemy in your dad's army. But God's army fights Satan's army. God's army uses the Bible and prayer as weapons. Satan is mad because God's army beat his army when Jesus died and rose again."

Grandma continued, "Now Satan goes around trying to keep people from knowing Jesus. When you become a member of God's family, you enter God's army. Groups of God's people praying for the same thing creates an army of prayer. And as we pray, God does amazing things."

The Bible tells what happened when God's people worked together in prayer. Once a big wall circled the outside of a city called Jericho. God's people were kept out of the city. It was a place of sin and evil. But God wanted Jericho to be his place.

God told his leader, Joshua, "Lead your army in a prayer march around the city one time each day for six days. On the seventh day, march seven times." A horn was to be sounded as Joshua called out to God's army. Everyone gave a shout and the city walls began to crumble. God's people were able to take over the city! And it all happened because of prayer.

Your Turn

1. What could happen if you prayed for your city?

_____

_____

2. Is your city God's place?

_____

_____v

Prayer

Dear God, make my city a place for you. Help me tell others about you so my city can be changed. Let my friends and neighbors know you. Amen.

My City Wall

Write the name of your city on the wall. List names of neighbors who don't know Jesus. Pray for them each day!

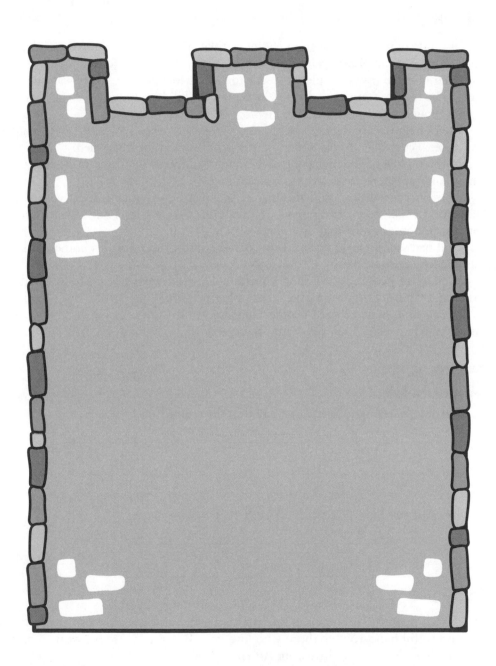

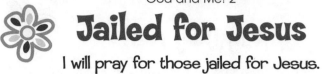 # Jailed for Jesus

I will pray for those jailed for Jesus.

Pray for those who persecute you.

~ Matthew 5:44

Needed Prayers

In most countries people go to jail for terrible crimes such as hurting or killing others. But in some places, people are sent to jail just for loving Jesus.

Even in Bible times people were sent to jail for loving Jesus. Peter was one of them. The king not only jailed Peter, he wanted to kill him because he was telling people about Jesus.

Peter's friends were worried about him. So they started to pray that Peter would be set free. Peter's friends didn't stop praying until something happened.

In the middle of the night one night, a man suddenly appeared in Peter's cell. The chains on Peter's arms and legs broke off.

"Put on your shoes," said the man. "And wrap your coat around yourself." Suddenly, the jail door swung open! The man and Peter walked out of jail! When Peter turned around, the man was gone.

God had sent an angel to free Peter. A friend took Peter into his house until it was safe for Peter to travel.

Even today, people are hurt and sometimes killed for loving Jesus. In places like Africa and China, God's people are jailed or harmed for being part of God's family. God wants us to pray for these people. God also wants us to pray for those who are hurting God's people. They need our prayers today!

Your Turn

1. Why are people who love Jesus hated in some places?

_____

_____

2. How can you help people jailed for loving Jesus?

_____

_____

Prayer

Dear God, help those who are in jail for saying they love Jesus. Lord, I ask for your powerful hand to save those who love you. Be with the men, women and children everywhere who love you. Amen.

Jailhouse Prayers

Draw someone in the jail cell below and create the bars on the jail cell. Use the prayers below to guide you as you pray with your family for people being jailed for Jesus.

Some ways you can pray for those who are jailed or harmed for loving Jesus:

God, comfort the families of those who are in jail or harmed.

I pray for those whose property has been destroyed and burned.

I pray most of all that God would be with his people everywhere.

I pray for the people in charge of countries where people are jailed for loving Jesus.

I pray you would place peace in their hearts and that they will come to know you.

Ways to Pray Each Day

I can find a place to pray.

When you pray, go into your room, close the door and pray.

~ Matthew 6:6

Every Step a Prayer

"I found a great place to pray, Mom," said Karla as they drove home from dance class.

"Where?" asked Mom.

"At dance school! Everyone is dancing and nobody is watching me," said Karla. "My Sunday school teacher told me to find ways to pray each day. She said to pray where you are. It doesn't matter where you are or what you're doing. So I pretend to create steps that go around the world. Then I pray people around the world will know Jesus. I make every step a prayer. "

"How do you do that?" Mom asked Karla.

"I'll show you," said Karla. "First I step to Mexico and pray for poor children. Then I step to Costa Rica and pray for our missionaries there. Next, I dance to South Africa to pray for peace. Last, I step home and pray for my friends here."

Mom smiled at Karla. "That's great," she said.

"I also pray when I ride my bike," Karla added.

"Well, I guess any place is a good place to pray," said Mom. "Jesus said we should shut our door and pray in secret."

"Does that mean I shouldn't pray at dance class?" Karla asked.

"Not at all!" said Mom. "It just means that we shouldn't show off when we pray. Anywhere we choose to pray is good. The point is that we can talk to God anywhere and any time."

"And that's just what I want to do," said Karla.

Your Turn

1. Why do you think Jesus wants us to pray in secret?

_____

_____

2. Do you think God cares where you pray?

_____

_____

Prayer

Dear Jesus, I am glad you will talk to me in any place and any time. Help me never to "show off" when I pray. Amen.

A Dancer's Prayers

Follow the girl dancing below. Write one prayer request on the blank at each place where the girl moves.

_____

_____

_____

_____

_____

_____

Prayer Hunt

Jesus wants me to pray.

Ask and it will be given to you; seek and you will find.

~ Matthew 7:7

The Dog Bone

Suzie had a little dog named Cleo. Cleo loved to chew on doggy bones. Suzie and her brother hid Cleo's bones in the yard and watched Cleo search for them. Cleo dug and scratched at the dirt to get to the hidden bone.

Hiding the bone and waiting for Cleo to find it was fun for Suzie. She especially loved watching Cleo sniff by the fence post, deck and bushes for the bone. Once Cleo found where a bone was hidden, she dug for it. Cleo would seek and then find the bone.

She wanted to meet Cleo's needs by giving her a bone to chew. But she also wanted Cleo to work for the bone. God wants to give you what you need, too. But, sometimes he wants you to work for it. Jesus said, "Seek and you will find." To "seek" means to look for something. Jesus was saying you should seek what God has for you.

Praying is kind of like working for what you need from God. God's plan is for you to know him, but you must read the Bible and pray in order to learn. Praying and reading the Bible help you dig up the things of God. Then you can come to know him better.

Love, forgiveness, joy and caring are things you can find when you dig in God's Word. When you pray you will find answers to your questions and needs.

God wants what is best for you. Pray and read God's Word to hunt for what is best. Seek God and you will find him.

Your Turn

1. Why do you think God wants you to seek him?

_____

_____

2. Where do you think you should hunt for God's love?

_____

_____

Prayer

Dear God, thank you for your promise that if I seek you I will find you. Help me to be hungry for you like a dog is hungry for a bone. Amen.

My Dog Bone

Dig up the good things of God! Make a circle around the bones you should dig up to find God's best for you.

Prayer Walking

My feet can walk as I pray.

I will give you every place where you set your foot.

~ Joshua 1:3

Feet, feet, feet

In a country far away, there were no cities or towns. Land was wide and bare. God's people wanted to live where they could freely worship him. They wanted to settle and build houses for their families.

So God gave their leader, Joshua, a promise. "Get ready to cross over the Jordan River," said God. "I'll give you and my people the land you walk on. No enemy will be able to come against you. I will always be with you."

Then God told his people to be strong and brave. "Be careful to obey my commandments," said God. "The land where you set your feet will become your land. Anyone going to that place will know the land is my place."

This is a wonderful promise for you today. You can claim your school, home and playground for God. As your feet take you to school, pray for your classroom. Pray the kids in your class will know Jesus. Pray your teacher will love God and teach you good things. Pray as you slide, swing and climb. Walk from one end of the playground to the other. Ask God to protect the kids there. Pray that the families who go to school there will know Jesus.

Let your feet walk for God. Let every place your feet walk be God's place.

Your Turn

1. Why do you think God gave land to a group of people?

_____

_____

2. Where do you walk each day?

_____

_____

3. What land around you can you claim for God?

_____

_____

Prayer

Dear God, thank you for the promises you give us. Help me to claim my home and school for you. Amen.

My Prayer Walk

Make your own prayer walk. Draw pictures in the boxes along the street below. Let them show where your feet walk each day.

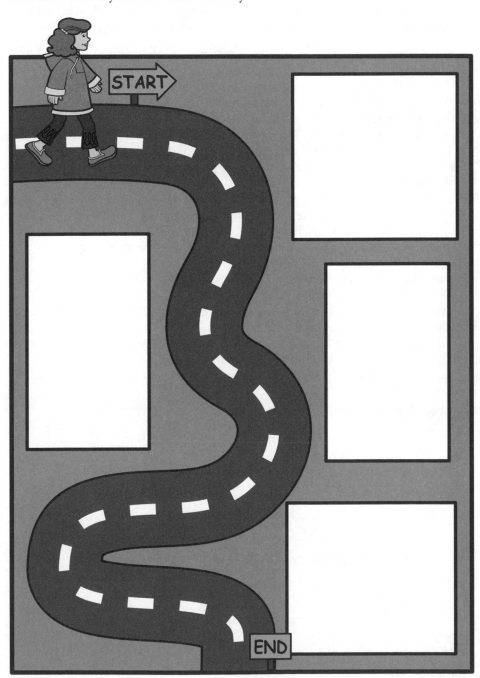

Pray or Complain

God wants me to pray, not complain.

Pray continually, give thanks in all circumstances.

~ 1 Thessalonians 5:17-18

Queen "C"

Jasmine stood on a stool at the kitchen sink. "Dishes, dishes, dishes. I hate doing dinner dishes," she complained.

Mom stuck her head around the corner of the kitchen. "Jasmine, are you complaining again?" she asked. "Remember what your dad and I told you: 'Pray and give thanks always.'"

Jasmine's family called her "Queen C." The "C" stood for "complainer."

"I don't like making my bed," Jasmine would say. "This milk is too cold." "This trash is too heavy." "I don't like this TV show." She always had something to complain about!

"I don't want to complain, but I can't stop," said Jasmine.

Mom told Jasmine, "There are people everywhere who don't have dishes to wash. They don't have a kitchen or enough food to eat. Some children don't have their own beds. They share with brothers and sisters because they are poor."

Jasmine looked sadly at the floor.

"Jesus wants us to be thankful always," said Mom.

"What do you mean by always?" asked Jasmine.

"'Always' means as often as you can," said Mom. "Stop each time you are tempted to complain. That's what the Bible says."

"I'd rather pray than be called Queen C anymore," sighed Jasmine. "I'll try harder. Praying before complaining will help me."

Mom smiled. "Praying before complaining will make you happier and God will be pleased, too."

Your Turn

1. Who pleases Jesus, a prayer or complainer?

_____

_____

2. Praying before complaining can make you happy. Why?

_____

_____

Prayer

Dear God, help me to remember to pray before I complain. Make me thankful for all I have. Amen.

A Queen's Mouth

Make a list of things you complain about inside the frowning and complaining mouth. Write "Thank you, God" inside the happy, praying mouth. Which mouth would please Jesus more?

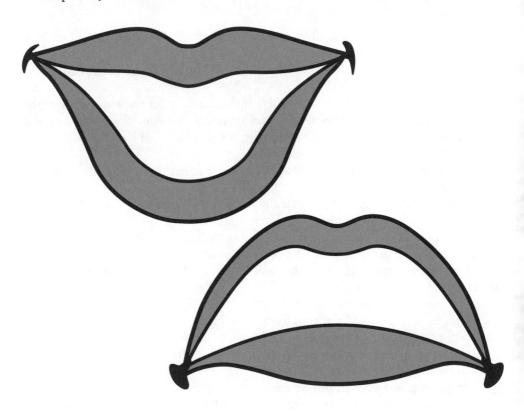

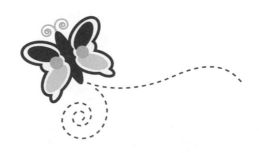

Stop, Drop and Roll!

I can roll my problems onto God.

Cast your anxiety on him because he cares for you.

~ 1 Peter 5:7

Roll It Away!

"Do you know what to do if your shirt catches fire?" Becca asked her family as they sat down at the dinner table.

"Of course I know what to do," said her older brother, Scott. "Everyone knows that you stop, drop and roll."

Becca looked surprised and disappointed that her brother knew the answer. She wanted to show off her knowledge of fire safety. Becca also wanted to share what she had learned in school that day. The firefighters from Station 11 had brought their truck and hoses to school to show the kids.

Everyone at dinner could tell that Becca was excited about what she had seen and heard.

"Okay, let's hear Becca share what she learned in school today," said Mom.

"Hmm," said Scott. "This will be interesting."

Mom poked Scott under the table. "Go on, Becca, tell us about it."

Becca cleared her throat. "Okay, well, stop, drop and roll can save your life. Never run when you catch fire," she said. "Instead, drop to the ground and roll around until the fire is out."

Dad waited until Becca was finished speaking. Then he said, "Stop, drop and roll works in prayer, too. When your feelings are hurt or if school becomes too hard, you might want to run away. But God doesn't want you to run away. Instead, he wants you to stop and drop to your knees in prayer. Then you can roll your troubles onto him."

"Stop, drop and roll can sure save us," said Becca.

"Yeah," said Scott. "It not only saves us from fire, but from our problems, too."

Roll your problems onto God. Just stop, drop and pray!

Your Turn

What happens when you stop, drop and roll in prayer?

_____

_____

Prayer

Lord, teach me to stop, drop and roll when I have troubles. You can put out the trouble in my heart. Amen.

Stop, Drop & Roll Chart

Use this page to create a stop, drop and roll chart. Under the stop picture, write the day's date. Under the drop picture, write the memory verse or another Scripture you like. Then under the roll picture, write your prayer request to God.

Together We Pray

God wants me to agree with friends in prayer.

If two of you on earth agree about anything they ask for, it will be done.

~ Matthew 18:19

When Friends Agree

Mrs. Phillips second grade class looked forward to Fridays. The afternoon recess was always long on that day. Kickball was their favorite class game.

At least it was the boys' favorite game. The girls didn't like it one bit.

So, just before a Friday recess, the girls decided to do something.

"We need to pick a girl to ask Mrs. Phillips if we can jump rope instead of play kickball," said Krissy.

"I think we should pick you, Krissy," said Casey.

"No, I don't want to ask," she told Casey. "Why don't you ask?"

Another girl named Kelly stepped forward. She put her hands on both girls' shoulders. "Why don't you go together and ask?" she suggested.

"Okay, let's talk to Mrs. Phillips together," Krissy said as Casey nodded in agreement. Then the two of them marched right up to their teacher.

When Mrs. Phillips heard what they wanted to do, she smiled. "If you want to jump rope, we'll work it out," she said.

The girls were glad that they decided to talk to the teacher together. Krissy and Casey were stronger when they combined their efforts.

The Bible says, "If two of you on earth agree about anything you ask for, it will be done." God hears your prayers and he hears your friends' prayers. So, if you get together and ask together, you have double prayer!

There is greater power in your prayer when friends agree together. Get someone to pray with you and see what God will do!

Your Turn

1. What does the Bible say will happen when two people pray together?

_____

_____

2. Do you have a friend or family member with whom you can pray?

_____

_____

Prayer

Thank you, God, for promising to hear my prayers. Make me more like Jesus. Help me to find friends who will pray with me. Amen.

Jump Rope Prayers

In the center of the rope draw a friend with whom you can pray.

The Heart Check-up

I want a clean heart when I pray.

Search me, God, and know my heart.

~ Psalm 139:23

Test Your Heart

Stacey's parents were planning a birthday party for a child at the downtown mission. The little girl's father was out of work and the family had lost their home.

"Let me help with the party," begged Stacey. "I like going to the mission."

Stacey did want to help with the party. She prayed that she could go, but in her heart she hoped to get a gift for herself. She also looked forward to eating cake and ice cream. Stacey's prayers to help at the mission were selfish.

Alexandra came from a family who prayed. Sunday school teachers often called on her to pray aloud in class. The other kids thought of Alexandra as a prayer leader.

"God, I pray that kids everywhere will come to know you as Lord and Savior," she said in one prayer. "I thank You that the kids in this Sunday school class know you. I'm glad we aren't in darkness like other kids."

Alexandra liked praying long prayers. Being the center of attention made her feel good. Alexandra prayed for the wrong reasons. She prayed to get attention rather than to talk to God.

Remember to check your heart before you pray. God wants you to talk to him because he loves you. He wants you to pray with a heart toward him, not toward yourself. Before you pray, test your heart. Be sure you are praying for the right reasons!

Your Turn

1. How were Stacey and Alexandra alike?

_____

_____

2. What could you do before you pray to be sure your heart is clean?

_____

_____

Prayer

Dear God, please search my heart. Show me my selfishness before I pray. Help me to hear what you want me to pray for, not just what I want. Amen.

My Heart Test

Before you pray, test your heart. Solve the puzzle below. See what you are to do when you pray. The answer is on page 240.

A	B	C	D	E	F	G	H	I	J	K	L	M
1	2	3	4	5	6	7	8	9	10	11	12	13

N	O	P	Q	R	S	T	U	V	W	X	Y	Z
14	15	16	17	18	19	20	21	22	23	24	25	26

$$\overline{16}\ \overline{18}\ \overline{1}\ \overline{25}$$

$$\overline{6}\ \overline{15}\ \overline{18}$$

$$\overline{20}\ \overline{8}\ \overline{5}$$

$$\overline{18}\ \overline{9}\ \overline{7}\ \overline{8}\ \overline{20}$$

$$\overline{18}\ \overline{5}\ \overline{1}\ \overline{19}\ \overline{15}\ \overline{14}\ \overline{19}$$

Pray, Girls, Pray

I will pray at all times.

Evening, morning and noon…he hears my voice.

~ Psalm 55:17

Creative Prayers

"Our friends the Millers are going to Africa," said Mom. "Dr. Miller is going to be a missionary there. That means your friend Sarah will be moving, too."

"Oh, I'll really miss Sarah but I'll pray for her while she's gone," said Sharice.

Sharice knew God wanted her to pray for others. Her family prayed at the dinner table and at bedtime. But God had given her the desire to pray at other times, too.

"Mom, can you help me make time to pray?" Sharice told her mom.

"Honey, you have time to talk to God even when you're busy," said Mom.

"When and how?" Sharice asked. Mom led her to the daily schedule sheet stuck to their refrigerator door.

"Let's look at your days," said Mom. "Do you take a shower each day? You can pray while you are in the shower. You can also pray while you are doing your chores. While helping me fold clothes, you can pray with me for each family member. In setting the table, we're reminded of families who have no food to eat. That would be a good time to pray for the poor."

Sharice had an excited look on her face. "I guess I'll need to get a little more creative," she said. "I am probably missing many chances to pray as I go about my day."

Talking to God through prayer is a way of showing love for one another and for God. The Bible says to pray for one another at all times. God loves when you pray. Get creative and think of ways to pray each day.

Your Turn

1. Are there activities you do each day when you can pray?

_____

_____

2. Tell God your new plan to pray each day.

_____

_____

Prayer

Thank you, God, for loving me and wanting to talk to me. Give me creative ideas for praying each day. Help me to make prayer a habit. Amen.

Creative Prayer Snapshots

Look at the prayer pictures in the boxes below. Write below each one what you could pray when you do that activity. For the last box, think of your own activity to use as a prayer time. Draw a picture of it.

Prayer Works

Praying makes things right.

When I am in distress, I call to you.

~ Psalm 86:7

Praying Through Trouble

Haley and Katie were playing dress-up. They took earrings and necklaces from Haley's mom's jewelry box.

While Haley was swinging a pearl necklace, the string snapped and the beads flew everywhere. Pearls soared from one end of the room to another.

"Oops…we're in big trouble," said Haley as she quickly tried to pick up the pearls scattered on the bedroom floor.

"Quick, shut the door," whispered Katie.

"Do you think anyone saw us?" asked Haley.

"No," said Katie, "but I feel very bad right now. Jesus knows what we did, but if we tell your mom we'll get into big trouble."

Haley knew in her heart what to do. "Shouldn't we pray and ask Jesus?" she asked her friend.

The girls held hands and asked for God's help. Katie stopped in the middle of their prayer. "I know what God wants us to do," she said.

"I think I know what you're going to say," said Haley. "We need to tell my mom what we did."

"Then we need to get the necklace fixed," added Katie.

Haley smiled. "That's so cool! God told us the same thing."

"Could we pray again to ask God to help us tell her?" asked Katie.

The girls prayed as they walked toward the room where Haley's mom was ironing. The girls took a big breath and told her everything. Haley's mother was not happy with the girls, but she forgave them. The girls used their own money to get the necklace fixed.

Prayer made everything turn out right. It's best to pray first–it always works!

Your Turn

How can prayer help you?

_____

_____

Prayer

Thank you, Jesus, for helping when I'm in trouble. Thank you for helping me when I sin. I'm glad you forgive me and help me to do right. Amen.

Prayer Pearls

Put the necklace back together by adding pearls in the missing spots. Use the line of pearls below the necklace to write something you did that got you into trouble. Did you remember to pray?

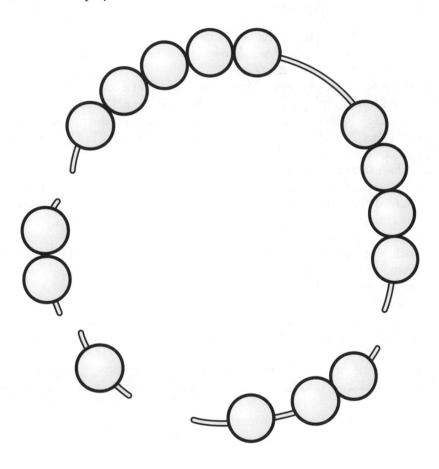

Tree Climbing

Prayer shows me things I can't naturally see.

Open my eyes that I may see wonderful things in your law.

~ Psalm 119:18

Seeing From Above

Abby loved climbing trees. Her two older brothers had taught her well. Besides, she was a bit of a tomboy. Abby was known in her neighborhood as the tree kitty. She could climb trees as well as any cat.

"Come down from that tree!" Mom would say. "You'll break your neck."

But even Mom's scolding didn't sway Abby's climbing. Peering high above the ground, she could spy everything: fire stations, churches and the grocery store, too.

"But, I feel like Zacchaeus!" Abby told her mom. "Tell me that story again, Mom."

"Zacchaeus was a tax collector and a little man who climbed a tree," said Mom. "Jesus was coming to town and he wanted to see him. But he was too short to see over the crowd. So he had an idea like yours, Abby. He ran ahead to where Jesus was going. He climbed up into a tree. He waited for Jesus to come that way. As Jesus approached the tree, he stopped.

"Looking up into the tree, Jesus saw Zacchaeus. 'Zacchaeus!' He called. 'You come down. I want to eat at your house tonight.' Zacchaeus came down and welcomed Jesus into his home.

"The people following Jesus weren't happy. Zacchaeus had cheated many people out of money. But now Zacchaeus wanted to change and live for Jesus. 'Lord,' he said to Jesus. 'I'll give part of what I owe people to the poor. Those people I cheated I'll pay back.'"

The stories of Abby and Zacchaeus are like prayer. When you pray, it's like climbing a tree to see Jesus. Prayer shows you things about God and Jesus you can't naturally see.

Abby had to climb the tree to see the church from her yard. Zacchaeus had to climb the tree to see Jesus. You also should pray to keep Jesus in your view. Prayer can keep you from losing your way.

Your Turn

Who keeps you seeing the right things when you pray?

_____

_____

Prayer

Dear God, help me see you and Jesus. Teach me to pray so I can see what you have for my life. Amen.

The Prayer Tree Maze

If you want to see who Jesus is, climb down from the prayer tree below. Find your way through the tree to see Jesus. Draw a line from the top of the tree to where Jesus is.

The answer is on page 240.

Puzzle Answers

page 11
God loves me!

page 15
Don't kick

page 17
Let us draw <u>near</u> to God with a sincere <u>heart</u>.

page 33

C R K W (I S) A
S O M H N E Y
(G O N I N Z D
U O P T P D O
W C (D A T) H S
R L Q K J O T
(W O R K) Z V L

page 73
Buckle up with the <u>belt</u> of <u>truth</u>.

page 85
1. Ruth
2. Hannah
3. Rahab
4. Jochebed
5. Anna

page 93
How many books are in the Bible? 66
Hide God's Word in your <u>heart</u>.
How many books are in the New Testament? 27
King David wrote the book of <u>Psalms</u>.
Matthew, Mark, Luke and John are called? The Gospels

page 103
Lord, You know all things.

page 107
mercy

page 111

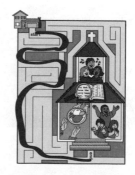

page 71

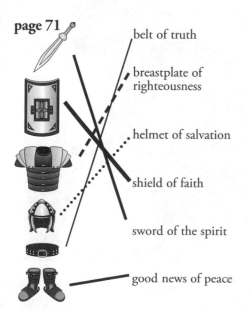

belt of truth

breastplate of righteousness

helmet of salvation

shield of faith

sword of the spirit

good news of peace

page 121
Love Jesus

page 125
I am with you always.
Matthew 28:20
I am the way, the truth and the life.
John 14:6
I will give you rest.
Matthew 11:28

page 133

page 147

page 151
Jesus Saves

page 159
Psalm 24:7/King of Glory
Psalm 80:1/Shepherd of Israel
Isaiah 9:6/Prince of Peace
Job 37:23/The Almighty
2 Corinthians 1:3/God of all Comfort
Joshua 24:19/Holy God
Isaiah 40:28/Creator

page 169
1. God
2. hurt
3. Tell
4. Jesus
5. go
6. Jesus
7. Give

page 185

page 199

page 231
Pray fir the right reasons.

page 237